In Winter Snows

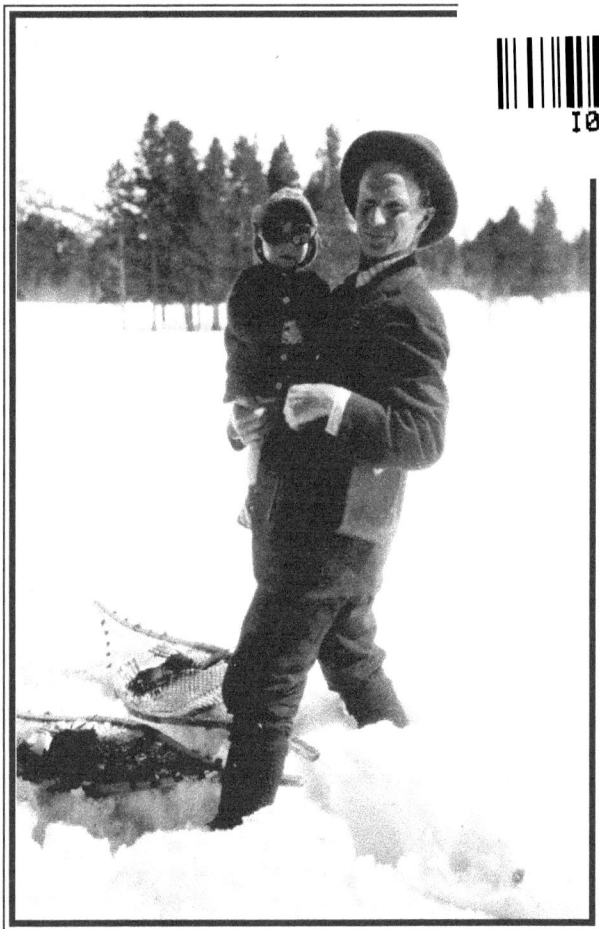

with best wishes of
Enos A. Mills

Edited by Elizabeth M. Mills and Eryn V. Mills
Temporal Mechanical Press
Long's Peak, Colorado

Contents

Thinking starts us on an endless quest.
John Burroughs

Introduction

The anticipation, the delicious whiffs of it in the air, the taste of the breeze, the tonality of the gray of the clouds, the clean frostiness of the wind, *Bon Hiver!* Good winter! The first show of snow crystals floating in free fall, makes my spirit smile and leap with light feet. I want to join in, gliding, flying, swirling and soaring in the air currents as this part of the planet refurbishes into a miniature Snowball Earth. Atmospheric conditions creates a physical reaction in me that I have no control over. Electricity in my brain takes over, my attitude improves, my gratitude and pun levels rise when it's getting ready to snow, while it snows, while snow is on the ground or if I think of snow. Primeval peace, the lizard brain at home in the ancient snow crystals.

As one voyages around the sun, dwelling in one place, one picks up behaviors for surviving in a particular environment. One learns to use factual knowledge, all the basics of every science to make life less hard and smarter. The thought of a foot of Snow everywhere is fantastic enticement to get chores done in the warmth of summer when there's a foot of lovely flowers everywhere.

One tends to get inventive when everything is going consistently wrong in the increasing slowing down and brittleness of extreme negative temperatures, the brain, hopefully warm enough, will come up with logical, simple, workable solutions in intense situations. Snow, wind and cold are fantastic motivators for vanquishing fear and choosing intelligence when the other option is freezing, it demands brain work that usually builds self-reliance and character.

Growing up, my Dad spent summers preparing for winter, doing cold chores in the radiance of the sun, or changing over to a simpler, smarter method. One year he put in a wood cook stove in our little log cabin and started teaching me the internal bliss of making bread, like his French Canadian Micmac Mowack grandmother had taught him. My big muscular Daddy was so tender, reverent with the yeasty life forms that transformed into our yummy bread. To enter your home with the smell of fresh bread baking or food cooking, while it's snowing, is such an essential part of maintaining life's senses.

As the accumulating snow crystals organize on the ground and moving it becomes necessary, we try to encourage the snow to stay as long as possible yet out of the way, either through snow fences, tree limb wood-rows, rocks or depositing the snow in shady places, around the base of trees is always reciprocated by our stable, sky cleaning friends and understandably by planting more trees.

Being kissed by the snow brings the usual, now anticipated euphoria as it did as a child, with ethereal hands on joy. Life is extraordinary. However... a bit of human powered speed seems to greatly enhance the experience; skis, skates or sled is splendidly exhilarating, it's fun being a flying snowflake crystal. Feeling the atmosphere impacting skin, frosty air in your lungs, floating in the snowy crystalline powder, the rush of sliding surface and dashing scenery, the authentic business of living. That astonishing sensation of being alive, the thrill that everything is interesting and captivates your attention.

Jamais Vu is the temporary lack of memory of doing something that one has actually done hundreds or thousands of times before, like how to use a door, the opposite of *deja vu*. That's almost how it is out in the snow and ice, no memory of lessons learned and the self inflicted pain. Every moment is fresh and memories are of fading relevance. I rush right back out there for more with joy in my heart and a limp in my step.

The adventurous serenity of crystalline moments, entranced by the lilliputian paradigms created by an ancient nuclear furnace refracting and reflecting on each surface of crystal and ice, literally blinding with beauty. To bundle up and venture inside the window's curtain and gaze upon the intricate designs on the glass with the intense spectrum of colors that have been revealed over night with simple distillation from the atmosphere that is billion of years old...beyond comprehension...deep brain synchronization...gratitude a luxurious graceful consequence. Every day life is a choice, electrified with the dance of the universe, with the transcendent primordial snow crystals from the Ice Ages.

Elizabeth
Long's Peak

Foreword

My first memory of snow happened when I was three years old. My family lived in Denver, and when I went to sleep the night before, I had no notion of winter weather. When I woke, however, all of my world had been covered by a two-foot layer of snow like a carefully thrown fleece. My mother dressed me in my new blue snowsuit, with mittens and hat and boots. Without much warning, I was tossed from the doorway straight into the thick, amazing white stuff that obscured our yard. As surprised as I was, once I realized I was surrounded by the snow and only my head poked above its limits, I laughed and insisted that I be thrown in again and again.

The snow was magical for me that day. In that yard I had played summer running games, helped my mother plant seeds in the spring, rolled around and tossed the crackling autumn leaves, but it was the snow, and the sheer quantity of it, that had transformed my front yard into an entirely foreign land.

To this day, it is still the coming of a strong winter storm that I anticipate with a little more excitement than usual, as each winter around my home shows me new sights, gives me new sounds and new adventures. Over the years, of course, as anyone does, I've grown accustomed to the change of seasons, and each one has its own wonders. To this day, though, I listen for that gust of wind that heralds the winter snows.

We need not venture days or weeks on end outside, as Enos often did, to revel in the excitements and mysteries of the seasons. Sometimes all we need is a little time in familiar scenes made unfamiliar by an overnight storm, or an hour of silent snowfall when our neighbors are at rest, awaiting the break in the clouds.

This new compilation of stories, I hope, will tempt new explorations, awaken dusty memories, maybe foster some wonder. We live on a planet with an astounding array of climates, and every day can be either an adventure or a chore.

Eryn V. Mills, 2014

When you arise in the morning think of what a precious privilege it is to be alive – to breathe, to think, to enjoy, to love.
Marcus Aurelius

In All Weathers

The seasons for visiting National Parks are spring, summer, autumn, and winter! Morning, noon, the sunset hour, under the stars and with the moon—all times, each in its way, are good for rambling in these places of instruction and delight. I have climbed numerous peaks by moonlight and starlight, and have stood on the summit of the Continental Divide with the winter moon. Nature is good at all times. Rainy days, gray days, windy days, all have something for you not ordinarily offered. So, too, have the sunny winter days when upon the dazzling snow fall the deep blue shadows of the pines. Forget the season and the weather; visit the Parks when you can stay there longest.

One day heavy clouds rested upon the snowy earth around my cabin, nine thousand feet above sea level. In these, and in the falling snow, I started up the Long's Peak trail, in what now is the Rocky Mountain National Park. I wished to measure the storm cloud's vertical depth and to observe its movements. Only a ravine and instinct enabled me to snowshoe through the blinding, flying snow and almost opaque sheep's-wool cloud. The cloud was three thousand feet thick.

Suddenly, at twelve thousand feet, the depth of snow became markedly less. Within a few rods I burst through the upper surface of the cloud into brilliant sunshine! Not a bit of snow or cloud was there above this upper level.

From a high ridge I watched the top surface of the storm cloud as it lay before me in the sun—a silvery expanse of unruffled sea, pierced by many peaks. Half a mile above towered vast, rugged Long's Peak. Like a huge raft becalmed in a quiet harbor, the cloud sea moved slowly and steadily, almost imperceptibly, a short distance along the mountains; then, as if anchored in the center, it swung in easy rotation a few degrees, hesitated, and slowly drifted back. Occasionally it sank, very slowly, several hundred feet, only to rise easily to its original level.

With wonder I long watched this beautiful sunny spectacle, finding it hard to realize that a blinding snow was falling beneath it. Later I learned that this snowfall was thirty inches deep over several hundred thousand square miles; but it fell only below the altitude of twelve thousand feet and not on the high peaks.

Mountaintops have more sunshine and fewer storms than the lowlands. The middle slopes of a peak regularly receive heavier falls of rain and snow than does the summit.

The rugged mountains in all Parks are wonderful in the snow. Snowshoe excursions, climbs, skiing—all the sports of winter—may be enjoyed in these magnificent wilds. Mountains in winter hold splendid decorations—sketches of black and white, ice architecture, rare groups that form a wondrous winter exhibition. Forests, canyons, meadows, plateaus and peaks, where hills of snow and gigantic snow canyons form dazzling structures and new topography, are marvelous exhibitions. The thousand and one decorations of frost and snow flowers are treasures found only under the winter sky.

During a high wind one winter, as I fought my way up Long's Peak, above timberline I was pelted with gravel and sand till the blood was drawn. The milling air currents simply played with me as they swept down from the heights. I was knocked down repeatedly, blown into the air, and then dropped heavily, or rolled about like some giant's toy as I lay resting in the lee of a crag. Standing erect was usually impossible and at all times dangerous. Advancing was akin to swimming a whirlpool. At last I reached the buzzing cups of an air meter I had previously placed in Granite Pass, twelve thousand feet above sea level. This instrument was registering the awful wind speed of one hundred and sixty-five miles an hour! It flew to pieces later during a swifter spurt.

Although I intended going no farther, the wild and eloquent elements lured me to keep on to the summit of the peak, nearly three thousand feet higher. All my strength and climbing knowledge were necessary to prevent me from being blown into space. Gaining each new height was a battle. Forward and upward I simply wrested my way with an invisible, tireless contestant who seemed bent on breaking my bones or hurling me into unbanistered space.

In one rocky gully the uprising winds became so irresistible that I had to reverse ends and proceed with feet out ahead as bracers and hands following as anchors. There was no climbing from here on: the blast dragged, pulled, and floated me ever upward to the sunny, wind sheltered Narrows. The last stretch was a steep icy slope with a precipice beneath. Casting in my lot with the up-sweeping wind, I pushed out into it and let go. Sprawling and bumping upward, I had little else to do but guide myself. At last I stood on the top and found it in an easy eddy—almost a calm compared to the roaring conditions below. Far down the range great quantities of snow were being explosively hurled into the air, then thrown into spirals and whirls that trimmed the peak points with gauzy banners and silky pennants, through which the sunlight played splendidly.

Stirring and wild, wonderful scenes are encountered during storms on mountaintops, by the lakeshore, and in canyons. The dangers in such times and places are fewer than in cities. Discomforts? Scarcely. To some persons life must be hardly worth living. If any normal person under fifty cannot enjoy being in a storm in the wilds, he ought to reform at once.

In the intensity and clash of the elements there is a vigorous building environment. The storms furnish energy, inspiration, and resolution. There are no substitutes "just as good," no experiences just as great.

One rainy June day I started up a dim steep trail toward the headwaters of the river St. Vrain, near timberline in what is now the Rocky Mountain National Park. While enjoying the general downpour and its softened noise through the woods, I was caught in a storm center of wrangling winds and waters, and was almost knocked down. Like a sapling, I bowed streaming in the storm. Later, as I sat on a sodden log, reveling in the elemental moods and sounds, a water ouzel began to sing, but I heard little of his serene optimistic solo above the roar of the wind and stream.

The storm raged louder as I approached timberline. Clouds dragged among the trees. I could see nothing clearly. Every breath was like swallowing a wet sponge. Then a wind surge rent the clouds and let me glimpse the blue sun-filled sky. I climbed an exceptionally tall spruce. A comic Fremont squirrel scolded in rattling, jerky chatter as I rose above the sea of clouds and trees. Astride the slender treetop, I felt that the wind was trying hard to dislodge me, but I held on. The tree quivered and vibrated, shook and danced; we charged, circled, looped, and angled.

Nowhere else have I experienced such wild, exhilarating joy. In the midst of this rare delight the clouds rose, the wind calmed, and the rain ceased. Then suddenly a blinding, explosive crash almost threw me from my observatory. Within fifty feet a tall fir was split to the ground. Quickly climbing back to earth, I eagerly examined the effects of the lightning stroke. With one wild blow, in a second or less it had wrecked a century-old tree.

Although I have rarely known lightning to strike the heights, I have frequently experienced peculiar electric shocks from the air. I have never known such electrical storms to prove fatal nor to leave ill effects; and they may be beneficial. The day before the famous Poudre Flood, in May, 1904, I was traveling along the Continental Divide above timberline near Poudre Lakes. While resting I was startled by the pulsating hum, the intermittent buzz-z-z-z and zit-zit and the vigorous hair-pulling of electricity-laden atmosphere.

Presently my right arm was momentarily cramped, and my heart seemed to lurch several times. These electric shocks lasted only about two seconds, but recurred every few minutes. The hair-pulling, palpitation, and cramps seemed slightly less when I fully relaxed on the ground. When I tried to climb, I found myself muscle-bound from the electricity. Points of dry twigs momentarily exhibited tips of smoky blue flame, and sometimes similar flame encircled green twigs below the lower limbs.

Later that day I came to North Specimen Mountain. There the electrical waves weakened or entirely ceased while I was in shadow, but they remained quite serious in the sun. I breathed only in gasps, and my heart was violent and feeble by turns. I felt as if cinched in a steel corset. After sundown I was again at ease and free from this strange electrical colic, which often worries or frightens strangers the first time they ex-perience it. I soon forgot my own electrical experiences in the enjoyment that night of the splendidly brilliant electrical effects beneath the enor-mous mountain range of cloud forms over the foothills. Its surface shone momentarily like incandescent glass, and occasionally down the slopes ran crooked rivers of gold.

I have had the good fortune to see geysers by sunlight, by moonlight, during gray stormy days, and also while the earth around them was

Skiers on their way from a geyser.

covered in snow.

By moonlight the mountainous National Parks are enchanted lands. There is a gentleness, a serenity, and a softness that is never known in daylight. Many a time I have explored all night long. The trail is strangely romantic when across it fall the moon-toned etchings of the pines. The waterfalls, crags, mountaintops, forest glades, and alpine lakes have marvelous combinations of light and shade, and they stir the senses like music. I wish that every one might see in the moonlight the Giant Forest in the Sequoia National Park, or timberline in the Rocky Mountain National Park. By moonlight the Big Trees will stir you with the greatest elemental eloquence. Those who go up into the sky on mountains in the moonlight will have the greatest raptures and make the highest resolves.

Miss Edna Smith is one of the most appreciative outdoor women I have ever known. Years ago I urged her to know the mountains at night. Here is one of her accounts of a night experience:—

At suppertime the chances seemed against a start. It was raining. Later the rain stopped, but the full moon was almost lost in a heavy mist and the light was dim. Mr. S. N. Husted, the guide, thought an attempt to ascend Long's Peak hardly wise. At eleven o'clock I went to Enos Mills for advice. He said, "Go." So we mounted our ponies and started, chilled by the clammy fog about us.

After a short climb we were in another world. The fog was a sea of silvery clouds below us and from it the mountains rose like islands. The moon and stars were bright in the heavens. There was the sparkle in the air that suggests enchanted lands and fairies. Halfway to timberline we came upon ground white with snow, which made it seem all the more likely that Christmas pixies just within the shadows might dance forth on a moonbeam.

Above timberline there was no snow, but the moonlight was so brilliant that the clouds far below were shining like misty lakes, and even the bare mountainside about us looked almost as white as if snow covered.

As we left our ponies at the edge of the Boulder Field and started across that rugged stretch of debris spread out flat in the brilliant moonlight, we found the silhouette of Long's Peak thrown in deep black shadow across it. Never before had that bold outline seemed so impressive.

At the western edge of Boulder Field there was a new marvel. As we approached Keyhole, right in the center of that curious nick in the rim of Boulder Field shone the great golden moon. The vast shadow of the peak, made doubly dark by the contrast, made us very silent. When we emerged from Keyhole and looked down into the Glacier Gorge beyond, it was hard to breathe because of the wonder of it all. The moon was shining down into the great gorge a thousand feet below and it was filled with a silvery glow. The lakes glimmered in the moonlight.

Climbing along the narrow ledge, high above this tremendous gorge, was like a dream. Not a breath of air stirred, and the only sound was the crunch of hobnails on rock. There was a supreme hush in the air, as if something tremendous were about to happen.

Suddenly the sky, which had been the far-off blue of a

moonlit night, flushed with the softest amethyst and rose, and the stars loomed large and intimately near, burning like lamps with lavender, emerald, sapphire, and topaz lights. The moon had set and the stars were supreme.

The Trough was full of ice and the ice was hard and slippery, but the steps that had been cut in the ice were sharp and firm. We had no great difficulty in climbing the steep ascent. We emerged from the Trough upon a ledge from which the view across plains and mountain ranges was seemingly limitless.

As we made our way along the Narrows the drama of that day's dawn proceeded with kaleidoscopic speed. Over the plains, apparently without end, was a sea of billowy clouds, shimmering with golden and pearly lights. One mountain range after another was revealed and brought close by the rosy glow that now filled all the sky. Every peak, far and near, bore a fresh crown of new snow and each stood out distinct and individual. Arapahoe Peak held the eye long. Torrey's Peak and Gray's Peak were especially beautiful. And far away, a hundred miles to the south, loomed up the summit of Pike's Peak. So all-pervading was the alpine glow that even the nearby rocks took on a wonderful color and brilliance.

Such a scene could last but a short time. And it was well for us, for the moments were too crowded with sensations to be long borne. Soon the sun burst up from the ocean of clouds below. The lights changed. The ranges gradually faded into a faraway blue. The peaks flattened out and lost themselves in the distance. The nearby rocks took on once more their accustomed somber hues. And in the bright sunlight of the new day we wondered whether we had seen a reality or a vision.

On the summit all was bright and warm. Long we lingered in the sunlight, loath to leave so much beauty, but at last we began the descent leisurely. It was a perfect trip. It seemed as if the stage were set for our especial benefit. It was an experience that will live with me always. At first I felt as if I could never ascend the peak again, lest the impressions of that perfect night should become confused or weakened. But I believe I can set this night apart by itself. And I shall climb Long's Peak again.

To enjoy the Parks, we need but to go to them realizing that these wilderness realms are the greatest places of safety on the earth. The thousand dangers of the city are absent; the altitude of high mountains is not harmful but helpful—the air is free from dust and germs; and even the wildest and most tempestuous weather within them will bear acquaintance.

The animals in the wilderness are not ferocious, and they wisely flee from the coming of Christian people. Extraordinary skill is required to get close to any wild animal. Even the camera will put the biggest wild folk to fright! They attack only in self-defense, only when cornered and assailed by the hunter. The animals that have survived and left descendants are those which used their wits for flight and not in ferocity. The grizzly constantly uses his wits to keep out of a locality where human beings are. Wolves may once have been ferocious, but at present the aggressive ones are those in the jungles of nature-faking; wolves keep apart from civilization, and travelers are not likely to go out of their way to find them. In storybooks the mountain lion crouches upon the cliff or lies in wait upon a tree limb to spring upon human prey; but real lions do not do this sort of thing.

Each year thousands of people scale peaks in the Rockies, the Sierra, and the Selkirks, or spend a less strenuous vacation in the heights, up several thousand feet above the sea. From anaemics who stay at home they hear the common superstition that altitude is harmful! But the travelers return to their homes in high hopes and in vigorous health. The heights are helpful, and the outdoors is friendly at all times. These are splendid sources of hopefulness. They "knit up the raveled sleave of care." They arouse new interests, give broader outlooks. They are great blessings that every one needs.

There is a growing appreciation of the safe and sane outdoors. People are rapidly realizing that vacations in the Parks and wild places are needful first aids to impaired health, and also that outdoor life is absolutely necessary for sustained or increased efficiency. From the wilderness the traveler returns a man, almost a superman. Its elemental songs, pictures and stories are a language of eloquent uplift. Go to the wilderness and get its good tidings! The wilderness is democratic and is full of ideas. It gives efficiency and sympathy. The mingling of all classes in the Parks is a veritable blessing; it is one of the greatest means of preventing internal strife and also of averting international war.

Nature is an educational stimulus of rare force. The crumbling cliff, the glacial landscape, the wild, free clouds, birds, and trees, compel children—old and young—to observe and think. They bring development and sympathy. They build the brain. They increase courage and kindness. Scenes and sunsets, cloud and storm, the stars and the sky, the music of wind and water, the purple forests, the white cascades, the colored flowers, the songs of birds, the untrimmed and steadfast trees, the shadows on the ground, the tangled grass, the round, sunny hills, the endless streams, the magic rainbow, and the mysterious echo—all these arouse thought, wonder, and delight in the mind of every child; and they have been the immortal nourishment of the great souls who have come from Mother Nature's loving breast to bless and beautify the world.

"The robe doth change the disposition." During summer vacations, the all-important rainy day costume will save endless disappointment and worry. Rainy days will bear acquaintance—if you have clothes for the occasion. Cheerfulness and rainy days are united by waterproofs. One simply cannot cheerfully face a rainstorm in clothes that water will ruin. Hats or shoes that go to pieces in a downpour, skirts with colors that run—these mean the Waterloo of some one when the rain comes down. But an inexpensive hat, strong boots, and a raincoat—then let it rain!

When one is in the woods, the foremost thing to remember is the direction back to camp. In a general way this is answered in the familiar caution: "Stop, look, and listen!" A traveler through the woods should occasionally stop and make sure of the direction in which he is traveling. At every important bend in his course he should look ahead and notice the most conspicuous landmark directly in front of him; then, about face for a look at the most important point or landmark that he has passed. He would thus be able, if he doubled on his own trail, to be guided by familiar objects, just as if he had traveled over it before in the same direction, with eyes open. Then, too, he should look to right and left for prominent or peculiar trees, cliffs, or other objects.

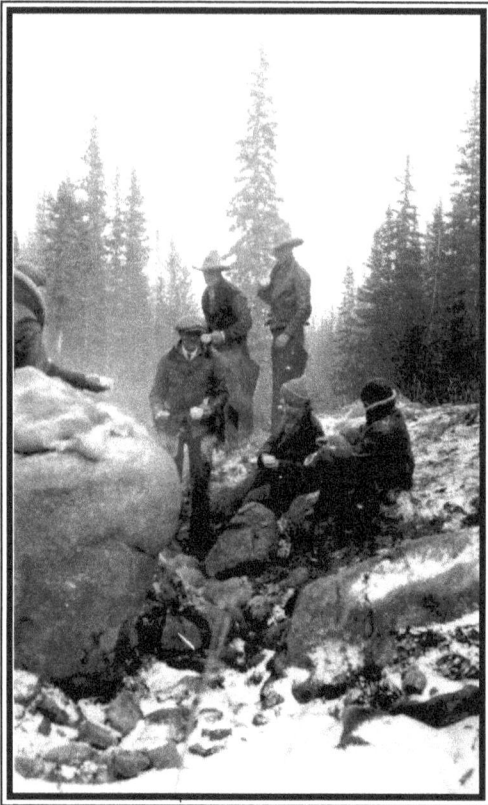

A group of
adventurous men
enjoy a winter
camp.

Keeping eyes thus open and mind alert is not a burden; it adds to the pleasure along the way. Any one who has thus traveled through strange woods should have taken a mental picture of what he has seen as he went on, and should be able to sit down and make a rough sketch of the locality and of his trail, showing the location of camp, the course he has traveled from it, and the prominent objects on both sides. A fair knowledge of woodcraft will enable any one to determine the points of the compass. While this is important, it is of less importance than remembering the direction to camp.

If a person gets lost, he would do well at once to climb into a treetop, or to the summit of the highest nearby place, and from the commanding height survey the surrounding country. This may enable him to see a familiar landmark. If he fails to recognize any point, let him make a comparatively small circle with the purpose of picking up his trail. He should be careful to avoid aimless wandering, to which often lost people are so prone. This he may do by following along the summit of a ridge, or down the first brook or stream he can find. Of course, he will keep downhill in looking for running water. A few hours, or at most a few days, of streamside travel will bring him where some one lives.

One is not likely to starve to death in the wilds. Starving is a slow process, and experiences show that a fast of a few days may be beneficial. Then, too, roots, berries, fruit, mushrooms, and tree bark are to be found. With nothing but these, I have repeatedly lived for two weeks or longer, even at times when I was most active in exploring or mountain climbing.

If a man is hopelessly lost, and if he knows that his companions are sure to look for him, he should stop right where he is when he finds that he is lost, and should camp and light two signal fires, giving a call at intervals.

Go into the Parks and get their encouragement. Among the serene and steadfast scenes you will find the paths of peace and a repose that is sweeter than sleep. If you are dulled and dazed with the fever and the fret, or weary and worn,—tottering under burdens too heavy to bear,—go back to the old outdoor home. Here Nature will care for you as a mother for a child. In the mellow-lighted forest aisles, beneath the beautiful airy arches of limbs and leaves, with the lichen tinted columns of gray and brown, with the tongueless eloquence of the bearded, veteran trees, amid the silence of centuries, you will come into your own.

Some time the grizzled prospector will lead his stubborn burro down the mountain and cease the search for gold; some time the miner will lay down his pick, blow out his lamp or his candle, and leave the worked-out mine; some time eternal night will come upon the gas- and coal-oil lamp; but our sunny hanging wild gardens—our Parks—are immortal; they will give us their beauty and their inspiration forever.

Esther Burnell Mills and Elizabeth Burnell, enjoying a day above timberline.

The waters may make the wonderful circuit through the clouds, the air, the earth, and the cells and veins of living things, any number of times – now a globule of vapor in the sky, now a starlike crystal in the snow, now the painted mist of a waterfall, then the limpid current of a mountain brook – and still the sea remains unchained.

John Burroughs

Launching Icebergs

One May, more than a quarter of a century ago, a whaling vessel lowered a boat, two Indians, and myself on the Alaskan coast supposedly by the entrance of the Muir Inlet. Rowing inland, we broke abruptly through the fog screen into the midst of a fleet of icebergs. Many were of stupendous size and several were of striking ice architecture. One pinnacled berg appeared like an enormous five-master. A majority of this strange fleet shone dazzlingly white in the morning sun, with blue-black shadows. There were stragglers, gray-black like colliers, and a few scattered ones of marvelous blue.

We pushed up the bay and presently were pulling to right and left among the icebergs putting out to sea, watching on our left the broken, bristling ice cliffs—the fronts of glaciers—against which the waves were washing. Occasionally, a heavy, towering mass of ice collapsed, creating terrific explosions in the water and sending rings of violent waves rushing toward every part of the bay. There was an almost continuous roar and splash of these heavy waves as they dashed upon the countless bergs scattered through the bay, causing them to rise and roll long after the wave had collapsed high up on miles of distant broken shore.

The Indians, munching fish eggs, watched the strange moving exhibit with interest, but fortunately with less enthusiasm than myself. Two heavy swells from launched icebergs rushed our boat and nearly spilled us as we swished over the top. The Indians insisted on our keeping about a quarter of a mile distant from cliff fronts, where bergs were launched and storm waves started.

However, we were caught by a danger unsuspected by the Indians

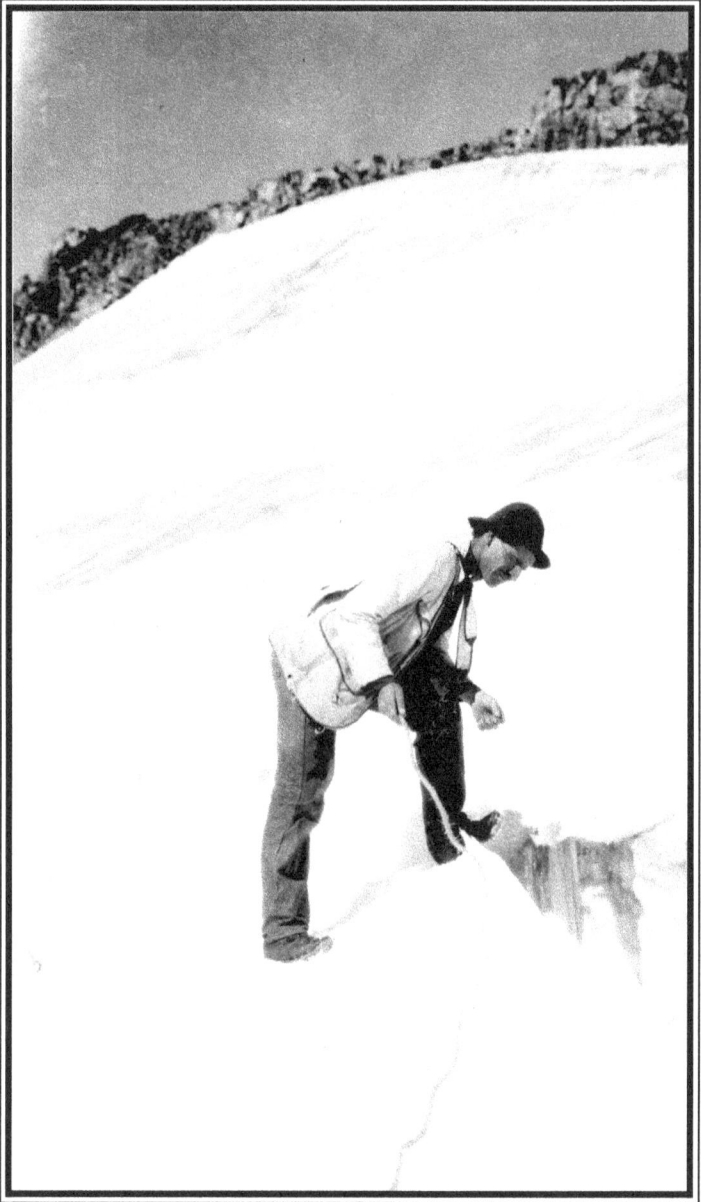

Enos explores a glacial crevasse.

and to me unheard of. We were headed for a distant inland channel, and several times dashed between close drifting bergs that threatened to crush us. We watched that these did not bow a shattered pinnacle upon us or that their falling ice chunks and boulders did not explode and deluge us with small fountains.

At last, we came into a stretch of open water. Not a wave was in sight, and a solitary big berg near us appeared asleep. Suddenly, we were lifted into the air upon upraised water, and for a moment looked down upon the top of this big berg. An enormous blue ice mass had broken loose from the depths and risen under our boat. Then we were swished shoreward on a wild, high wave, which flung us out of the bay.

We dragged our drenched selves from an alder thicket sixty feet above the shoreline. One of the Indians was still munching dried fish eggs. The alder clumps had been our shock absorber, but the boat had broken its head against one boulder and its back across another. Dripping, we three stood for a moment watching all our food and bedding floating off with the flotsam and jetsam of the bay.

The boat was smashed, the outfits a total loss; but flopping among the willows and alders were hundreds of fish, which were flung ashore by the wave that changed us to castaways. We built a driftwood fire among the alders and boulders, and as we steamed, we looked in and round the bay upon one of the grandest glacial exhibits in all the world. We had missed Muir Inlet, but had landed in the unrivaled Yakutat Bay.

The detached iceberg that wrecked us had risen from the bottom of the bay a thousand feet in advance of the visible front of the glacier. This submarine berg was a deep blue, but changed rapidly to white.

A number of the many glaciers that terminated in the bay were sliding in canyon channels which bottom a few hundred feet below water level, while the tops of their ice fronts stood two hundred feet above the water. That part above water level was cut off by wave action and detached as icebergs more rapidly than the submerged invisible part. Apparently, all blue bergs rose from the depths, and these changed rapidly to white. The gray-black bergs were masses of glacial debris—gravel and boulders.

This mountain-locked harbour appeared to contain all the glaciers and icebergs of creation. The mountain walls were so thickly, heavily laden with ice and snow that the rocks were only here and there visible. The adjacent white mountains send down mile-wide glaciers which terminate in this bay; launch ships of white—icebergs—which later go down to the sea.

I.C. Russel, the celebrated geologist and glaciologist, had explored this scene a year earlier, and Frederick Funston had landed somewhere in the region only a few days before me.

I was bound for the interior of Alaska, but thought to visit the Muir Glacier, in which Muir had interested me, while waiting for the excess of snow to clear from the Chilcoot Pass trail. My plan was to repair the broken boat and with this go for another and supplies. These could perhaps be obtained at the nearest Indian encampment. The two Indians said that with repair materials they could put the humpty-dumpty boat together again. All the remainder of the day, we three searched miles of shoreline among the boulders and alders, and that evening had a pile of fragments—broken boxes and their precious nails, rope, a few tin cans, and the green and invaluable skin of a wolf that had evidently been killed by a wave rush which crushed him against the boulders.

We broiled fish for supper and lay down without bedding between driftwood fires. The night was still except for the falling ice cliffs and the wash from their waves. The stars were near, and the snowy mountains made splendid marble architecture in the night.

Leaving the Indians struggling with the broken fragments of the boat, I next morning climbed a high, commanding point above the bay. Snowy mountains, glaciers, and icy peninsulas edged the water. Everything was on a stupendous scale. A wide canyon below me carried a glacier that extended miles and leagues back into the high white mountains. A snow slide gave an excellent exhibition by plunging down upon the glacier. The slide was so far away that I heard not a sound, but so large was it that its lurches, leaps, and curvings were easily seen. A thousand-foot column of agitated snow dust rolled up and stood briefly over its roughened mass, where this stopped half a mile out on the glacier.

One avalanche, a mixture of rocks, ice, and snow, started near me and crashed down upon the glacier. For longer than a minute, its echoes and reechoes rioted so vigorously among the snowy cliffs and icy canyons that I looked, expecting to see something in action. When the avalanche came to a stop out on the ice, the mass appeared as large as several

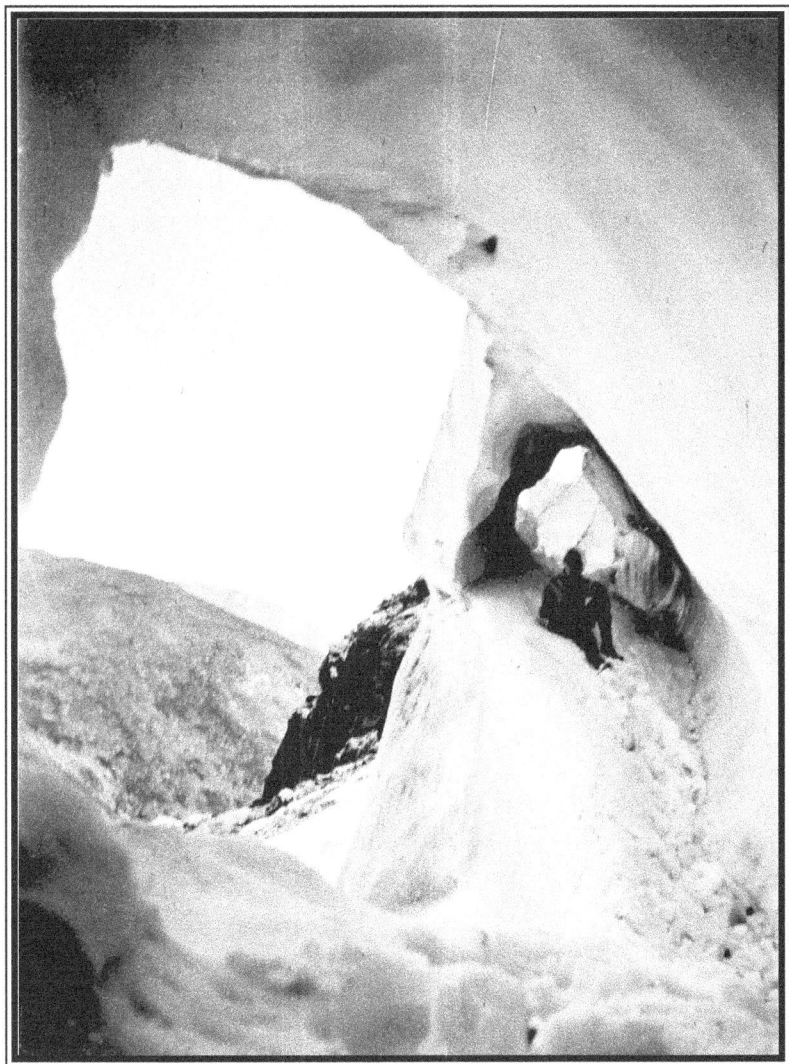

Relaxing in the edge of a glacier.

Mauretanias. So extensive was the scene that, when I lowered my field glass, I had difficulty in finding it with my good eyes.

Northward, as far as the eye could reach, was a vast desert of snow. Many mountains appeared to be made of it; others were deeply buried beneath it; and here and there the tip of a peak barely pierced its heavy stratum.

What an array of water in cold storage! A snow desert as large as two or three New England states, together with hundreds of square miles of ice. In due time, all this crystal cloud material would be shaped into finished products—icebergs. These would be launched by the glaciers, exhibited in the bay in front of the steep white mountains, then sent forth on a strange sea voyage to melt and mingle again with the waves and clouds.

Off in the distant west lay what I took to be the Malispina Glacier. It occupied an empire of surface and was so nearly stagnant that groves were growing in its debris-covered back.

The 2,000-mile stretch of Pacific Coast between the mouth of the Columbia River and Cooks Inlet, Alaska, has an extremely heavy snowfall: sixty feet a year and upward—mostly upward. The Yakutat Bay-Mount St. Elias region is laden beneath its full-heaped share. More snow falls each year than melts. The accumulating snow quickly changes to ice through compression and partial melting. As this ice mass becomes sufficiently weighty, it begins to crawl down slopes. It becomes a flowing ice river—a glacier.

Glaciers, like water rivers, move forward along the line of least resistance. The rate of movement depends on the weight of the mass, the degree of steepness and roughness of the slope down which it moves. Small and nearly stagnant glaciers advance from one to twelve inches a day, but the majority of glaciers go forward from one to ten feet a day. On rare occasions, a combination of favorable conditions may cause any glacier to lurch briefly and slide forward at greatly increased speed.

A few years ago, an earthquake in Alaska temporarily put new life into numerous glaciers. They were shaken out of slow-going ways. The Muir Glacier was shattered and changed by the quake. Its lower reaches slid forward and so jammed its terminal bay with icebergs that steamers were unable to enter the bay for two years. By the time the bergs had cleared, the end of the glacier had retreated and no long reached tidewater.

For a few days following the earthquake, a number of glaciers rushed ice deliveries— launched numbers of icebergs. This was followed by normal flow for some months; then an intensified, prolonged flow occurred, evidently due to the flood of glacial material—rocks, ice, and snow—which the earthquake had shaken down upon the source months before. These glaciers, one, two, and even three years after the quake, advanced, pushed their noses forward from a few feet to a quarter of a mile. This quake occurred a few years later than my visit.

I saw only one glacier that was advancing beyond its former terminus. It was one that melted away without reaching tidewater. Its thousand-foot front was ploughing through morainal deposits made years before. In places, this debris was nearly one hundred feet deep. Part of the moraine was covered with a spruce forest that was more than a century old. The crushed, cracking trees filled the air with the odor of balsam and pitch as the ponderous, irresistible mass pushed invisibly forward. In front of the ice mass, trees were leaning forward at every angle; numbers were uprooted, while others were down and the ice front sliding upon them. This forest now being flayed and crushed alive had grown in glacier-made soil—soil crushed and ground from rocks and distributed in other days by a glacier.

On the way back to camp, I walked two miles over the rough surface of the glacier on which I had seen the avalanche descend. One section evidently was above a rough, steeply inclined place in the bottom of the channel—a place that would create wild rapids in a river. The slow-advancing ice opened into crevasses as it passed over this place. An enormous pile of rock debris that was emptying into these crevasses had slid down upon the glacier more than a mile upstream. The time required to advance this far had probably been about two years.

A goodly quantity of this rock-slide debris had already dropped into the yawning crevasses. While I stood near, several large rock fragments from the pile tumbled in, and on the caving edge, small stuff was almost constantly sliding or tumbling in. Down in the glacier, these rocks would be pressed powerfully together. Numbers probably would drop to the bottom, where the glacier, with a few hundred tons' pressure, would ride and slide upon them, crushing and grinding them against the bottom and each other as the ponderous glacier moved ever forward.

A glacier is a sculptor of the rock ball called the earth, and it carves the surface into canyons and plateaus, making scenery and soil. At the source of a glacier, as well as at crevasses, ice, snow, sand, gravel, and slide rock accumulate and mingle in the upper end of the channel, and this confused mass of cutting tools tears and polishes the sides and bottom of the canyon channel as the mass slides forward. Not only is the channel widened, deepened, and straightened, but the tools themselves are mostly worn to dust by the time the terminus, or end of the glacier, is reached.

The last Ice Age made vast changes in the topography of the Northern Hemisphere. It ground up and moved mountains, changed river channels, made thousands of lake basins and fiords and covered thousands of square miles with productive soil. Glaciers—compressed snow flowers—carve grand scenery and soil. Much of the soil in the temperate zone is largely made up of rock flour of glacial manufacture. The surface of several Mississippi Valley states is deeply overlaid with glacier grindings, and most forests in the Rockies and in the Cascades and the Sierras are standing in glacial soil.

Returning to camp after a long day among glacial wonders, I found the serene Indians had made a start in assembling the fragments of our shattered boat. The repairs would require a few days longer to finish. As my assistance was declined, I took a hunk of broiled fish and set off for a two-day trip, hoping to reach the source of one of the glaciers. Among the willows by the lower end of the glacier near the bay, I found numbers of flocks of ptarmigan. A mile or so up the glacier on the south wall I saw a number of bighorn sheep.

This glacier was more than three miles wide and probably a thousand or more feet thick, and filled the bottom of a canyon from wall to wall. The snowy, icy walls rose, perhaps, two thousand feet higher. On top of the glacier, I walked eastward up this wild, white, wide avenue. The surface of the glacier, which appeared generally level, was mostly snow-covered. Most of the time, I was within a few hundred feet of the south wall, but kept this distance to be safe from falling rocks and down-rushing slides.

Another danger was from the snow-covered crevasses. Numbers of the wider and longer crevasses were either open or were separated by high, sharp ice ridges, which advertised the hidden dangers. In places, there would be a single narrow crevasse; in other places, half a hundred openings in close succession. Whenever there was any doubt, I explored with a long staff; but much of the time I was able to keep on the solid, snowless ice of windswept ridges, where there was no danger.

Mid-forenoon, a bear, evidently a grizzly, crossed the glacier from the south. I was in a hollow between snowdrifts and a crevasse, and he did not see me. When about a quarter of a mile out on the ice, he heard a snow-slide behind and turned to watch it. This slide was closely followed by a rock slide, which went down with a thunderous roaring and crashing. The grizzly watched it, rising on hind feet. As soon as the straggling tail-end fragments ceased coming down, he went to the rock wreckage and climbed over it. Here and there, he stopped to eat something, probably roots. Leaving the wreckage, he followed his tracks back to the spot where he had stopped, turned for another look, then shuffled across to the north side, where he disappeared among the rocks.

Often I turned aside to examine the enormous piles of avalanche rocks that lay upon the glacier, and I came upon one that was thirty-two steps long. It was embedded slightly in the ice, but rose at least thirty feet above ice level. This enormous rock was floating down on the ice stream as readily as a chip floats on water. Of course, its progress was slow. It evidently had been carried about one mile.

On top of this wide glacial highway, I walked inland over hundreds of piles of debris, some almost pure snow, others mostly rocks and earth. The spring thaw evidently was the time of snow and rock slides, as the thaw was releasing the rocks wedged loose during the winter and loosening the big, steep-placed snowdrifts. As I could see miles ahead, with no end of the glacier in sight after six hours' walking, I turned aside to explore the source of a small tributary glacier or ice river.

Glaciers begin abruptly, like a river which starts in full volume from voluminous springs. This small glacier filled a tributary canyon about a mile long, which ended abruptly against a 1,000-foot wall. Down this wall and from slopes to right and left came snow slides and rock slides. A score or more of these had piled their contributions in one mass of fierce confusion a little below the uppermost end of this glacier. Rocks, ice, snow—in a pile four hundred or more feet high—were settling into place, and in a short time would be blended and a part of the slow-moving ice river.

Glaciers, like rivers, cut headward with surprising rapidly. The high, precipitous will in front of the head of this glacier evidently was due to the headward undermining and backcutting of the glacier. The crack, or *bergschrund*, which commonly is open between the upper end of the glacier and the snowfield or rock wall, allows air—and with it changing temperature—to reach beneath the upper end of the ice. This air and changing temperature means freezing and thawing, rapid rock disintegration and separation. Often, the upper end of the ice freezes fast to loosened blocks of rocks. These are then slowly dragged out. Long's Peak, Colorado, has been half carried away by the headward cutting of a glacier. This attacked its east wall from the abutting end of a glacier-filled canyon at an altitude of about twelve thousand feet, twenty-five hundred feet below the summit. In the Big Horn Mountains, Wyoming, are remnants of former peaks, the remainder having been carried slowly away by back-cutting glaciers. Canyons now are where peaks formerly stood.

Leaving this glacier-forming place, I started on the return journey, hoping to reach the coast before night. During the afternoon, I went across the glacier to examine a peninsula-like ridge of ice that thrust in a quarter of a mile from the north wall, and with a surface a few hundred feet higher than the general level of the surface of the glacier.

Evidently, there was an inthrusting rock ridge in the bottom of the canyon, and over this rock ridge, or peninsula, the glacier river flowed; for glaciers, like water under pressure, will flow up a grade, or uphill. The glacier was simply flowing up and over this inthrusting obstruction in its channel.

Sunset hour, with its long, ragged lights and shadows, was on the glacier when I left this deeply crevassed, icy peninsula and started on. It would require two hours to reach the coast, and as this could not be made before dark, I began to watch for a place to camp, as it would be perilous to travel among the glaciers in the dark.

Up on the north wall, several hundred feet above the glacier, was a grove of Sitka spruces. A part of this grove had been recently cut away by a snow slide. The trees thus wrecked lay before me in confusion on the ice. Many of the trees were smashed to cordwood, numbers were buried end-on several feet in the ice. On a bed of boughs, between two roaring fires, I had a fairly comfortable, primitive night.

The following day I spent among the glacier end in the edge of the bay, with its fleet of bergs. The bay is the launching harbor of many glaciers. One of these glaciers, then unnamed, thrust out into the bay an ice front that was at least four miles wide and with ice cliffs more than two hundred feet high. Two other glaciers were more than a mile wide, together with numbers of smaller ones, a few of which melted away back from the shore, but which in former times had contributed ice ships to the waiting waters.

The entire front of a small glacier had recently slid into the sea. Its channel was a few feet above sea level. Standing in the rock channel by the broken ice front I could hear the grinding of rocks and ice as the ice slide invisibly forward. Beneath one edge of the front were massed several thousand boulders of assorted sizes. These were grinding against one another and the bottom. At one point, embedded in the ice front, was an angular, unworn rock fifteen or more feet long that had made a long journey without being forced against either the bottom or another rock, though other rocks had been ground to dust under terrific pressure.

Northward, across a narrow arm of the bay, a small glacier up in a hanging valley, the end of which was about one hundred feet above the water, discharged its icebergs with drop and splash into the bay. Hearing a crashing, I looked across in time to see an enormous ice chunk—it was the entire end of this glacier—tumbling into the bay. A gushing, enormous fountain of water shot up and a ponderous wave swept from it across the bay. This wave threw water over the Indian boat menders who were at work more than mile distant and one hundred feet above the shoreline. Near where I was standing, there came a wild rush of waves, logs, and small icebergs. These were flung upon the shore, and many left stranded from one hundred to one hundred and thirty feet above water level. It was the wildest wave that I have ever seen.

It was dark at the end of the second day when I reached camp. The cheerful Indians had fixed the boat and made an excellent paddle. The following morning they set off down the bay, hoping to find supplies and another boat in an Indian camp along the near coast. An inspector would not have given this repaired boat an A1 release, for in rough water it surely would have gone to pieces. Away went the Indians, with two or three broiled fish. I was not allowed to go along, because the craft was dangerously frail even for two. One Indian speeded with the paddle while the other necessarily bailed rapidly, and both were apparently indifferent to the fact that they were playing with death. I planned to remain close to camp, as the Indians felt they would find necessities and return that night.

During the morning, I wandered a few miles southward along the now famous Russell Fiord. It was up this fiord that the Harriman party steamed a few years later. During the afternoon I strolled the shore, watching some of the numerous moving glacial actions. One of the best exhibits of the day was given by a hulk of a flatboat-like iceberg that was top-heavy and tilting with a mass of boulders and other glacial debris. It was dark enough for a collier. It came in sight from behind other bergs, drifting down the bay, with parts of its cargo occasionally dropping overboard. In passing near me, it struck an invisible obstruction and gave a lopsided lurch, dumping most of its cargo into the bay. the dumping of debris, the filling of the bay, was steadily going on.

This berg, an instant after dumping, rolled back and came near to turning a side turtle. Shaking itself as it rolled about, it finally turned end for end. Then this rudderless fresh ice hulk was caught in the outgoing tide and set off for a vanishing voyage somewhere out in the wide salty sea.

Most glaciers over the earth have been shrinking during the last two decades. This shrinkage is due either to lessened snowfall or to a slight warming of the glacier regions. Of all the remaining glacial regions of the world, it is doubtful if any excel the wonderful one round Yakutat Bay.

Glacial debris in inconceivable quantities, with embedded logs, strewed or formed every shore of the bay. One stretch of the shoreline had been recently uplifted by internal earth movements—this was about twenty feet above its former level—while another stretch showed subsidence of several feet. At one place, a grove just submerged was being battered away by the waves.

On the shore, on moraines, and in detached places on the mountainsides, were groves of Sitka spruce and growths of arctic willow and alder. I saw many kinds of wild flowers and numerous species of migrating birds. Resident gulls and ptarmigan were plentiful.

During the calm, clear evening I built a bonfire of extravagant proportions. I was determined to give welcome to the Indian rescuers if any returned—the warmest welcome possible for a castaway. As I sat by the fire, I could hear the splash of falling ice cliffs and the never-ending wash and dash of ice-sent waves against shores near and far. Shortly after midnight two boats rowed into the outer edge of my bonfire light.

Three hours later, two boats, four Indians, and I were dodging icebergs down the bay.

One of the large bergs had a number of spruce logs half embedded in it. These thrust from the sides and the top. Flocks of birds rested on these logs. The Indians said that birds sometimes nested on icebergs that floated about in the bay.

We landed on the main coast for the night. While busily engaged in making camp in the edge of a dense, damp spruce forest, a small steamer rounded a forest point about a quarter of a mile down the coast.

After a deal of shouting and signaling, we attracted attention, and in due time I was on board, with the two Indians who took me into the bay and who were to be with me during the summer.

The steamer had brought a number of enthusiastic prospectors and their outfits and put these ashore. Alaskan prospectors were increasing in numbers. Two days later, the two Indians, several hundred pounds of supplies, and I were put ashore at the foot of Chilcoot Pass trail, the trail which became famed a few years later during the strange, intense gold-seeker's rush.

Those who dwell among the beauties and mysteries of the Earth are never alone or weary of life.
Rachel Carson

Coasting off the Roof of the World

At four o'clock on a clear, cold February morning I left my cabin with a pair of bear-paw snowshoes under my arm, a hatchet on my belt, kodak, field glass, thermometer, a few pounds of raisins, and elkskin sleeping bag. My cabin was on the eastern slope of the Continental Divide at nine thousand feet, and about twelve miles from the summit. I was off to explore the winter summit of the Divide, to see the snow and ice fields, frozen lakes, and also to have a look at the winter ways of birds and animals that lived on the top, from twelve to thirteen thousand feet above sea level. Being alone I might hurry along and make the other side by night or might go leisurely, stopping to watch animals or turning aside for a look at anything that interested me.

The first welcome delay came when a few miles from my cabin. Eighteen mountain sheep, single file, came suddenly out of the woods. They broke into a racing, romping gallop and scattered toward a frozen over water hole. Eagerly they licked up the salty, alkaline dust around the shore. Three little lambs stuck out their tongues, smelled the ground, tasted it indifferently, and then began to play. By and by pairs of the older sheep played. They jumped, butted, and, standing on hind legs, fenced lightly and in a lively manner with their horns.

Large holes had been licked into the earth around this alkaline ooze to the depth of two or three feet. Sheep, like most other hoofed animals, appear to be fond of salt and make long journeys for it. These sheep lived on Battle Mountain above timberline, about five miles from this water hole.

After watching this flock for some time I started on for the top. There was no snow around, and the sunny day was warm as is common for many of the winter days in the Rocky Mountains. It was a warm climb up the steep slope. I looked back down the slope with my field glass. The old sheep were lying in the sunshine and the three little lambs were racing

Enos adjusts his snowshoes.

back and forth across the grassy opening which was enclosed by pines.

From the top of a bluff I looked down upon a beaver colony. Several ice-bound ponds were shining in the sun. Climbing down to them I walked across the main pond. A large house, recently plastered, thrust up five feet through the ice. The four or five inches of mud and small sticks on the outside of the house were frozen as solid as stone. There was no sign that any animal had tried to break in through this covering. Nearby a green brush heap stuck up through the ice. This brush pile, made up perhaps of two hundred small aspen trees, was the winter food supply. It rested on the bottom of the pond—was canned in the water. A beaver under the ice easily drags one of these green sticks from the food pile to his house entrance, also on the bottom of the pond, and then up to the floor of the house which is just above waterline. Rabbits hopped about in the shadows eating willow bark, but no other animals were in sight.

A climb of about a thousand feet above the beaver colony, through a dense, tall spruce forest, brought me to timberline. This timberline was a stretch of forest less than three feet high which appeared to have stood here al long as the peaks themselves. That each of these ancient looking trees was hundreds of years old is certain. Farther along the timberline the trees lay upon the ground as though they had been flattened out by a steam roller. A few of these were about one foot in diameter and twenty feet long. Here and there a badly windblown tree, with a thin spread of limbs on just one side, looked like a flagpole waving a tattered green banner. The windward side of the trunk was bare. In other places there were clumps of low growing trees with their limbs entangled so thickly that the sunlight and the wind could scarcely break through.

One tree clump was deeply set in snow. It was as though a heavy white canvas had been spread over with one side left open. This was the place for me to spend the night. In similar, though better-covered places, many a bear has hibernated. In I pushed my sleeping bag. The night was cool, my thermometer showing ten degrees above zero, but so snug was this shelter that I slept on my sleeping bag and not in it. My fire was not a large one, but was arranged with backlogs which reflected a part of the heat into my almost windproof shelter.

These trees were 11,300 feet above sea level. This is 5,000 feet, almost a mile, higher up the mountain side that timberline in the Alps. In the Alps there is more snow and more cold, cloudy days. But the Rocky Mountains, having many warm, sunny days, provide a tree-growing climate and a place for plants and birds and animals to live a mile farther up into the sky than they can in the Alps.

A short distance from my timberline camp the next morning I came to the largest icicle I have ever seen. It overhung a cliff and must have been two hundred feet high. At the top it was twenty feet or more in diameter. The lower and stood on an icy foundation that overspread the rocks. While I was looking at a number of smaller icicles one broke away and fell with a crash. Chunks of this icicle as big as a huge barrel went rolling and bounding down the mountainside, one piece remaining unbroken until it crushed into the tree tops at timberline.

Snow covers small streams and protects them from freezing, preventing ice forming and filling in their channels. During a winter of but little snow on mountaintops many a spring overflows its ice-filled channel. Climbing to the top of the cliff to which these icicles hung, I found a great fanlike span of ice over the surface. This was about three hundred feet wide at the face of the cliff. There was a spring at the point of the "V" or fan, some five hundred feet up the slope. Without snow to protect this spring water, it had frozen until the channel was filled with ice. Then the water had overflowed, spreading and freezing wider and deeper. This fanlike span of ice had taken about three months to form and in places was several feet deep. Over the face of the cliff were icicles of all sizes, many beautiful columns, and many other attractive ice formations.

Farther up the slope I came upon a flock of ptarmigan—"white quail." They allowed me to come within a few yards of them without showing alarm. They were white, wore white leggings, were nearly as large as prairie chickens, and made a showy appearance as they walked along the brown, bare earth. Three of them flew a short distance and alighted on a nearby snowdrift. They matched the snow so well that I lost sight of them the instant they alighted. A quarter of a mile below the summit of the almost level mountain top a flock of sheep watched me pass within two hundred feet without alarm or retreat.

At last I stood on the very top of the Continental Divide and faced the noonday sun. I stretched out on the bare granite with my head and shoulders on the Atlantic slope and my feet on the Pacific slope. I remembered reading years before that one of the members of the Lewis and Clark exploration party had enjoyed standing for a minute with one foot on one side of the Missouri River and one on the other side. He was standing near the top of the Continental Divide where the stream began.

I stood 12,500 feet above sea level and looked back down the Atlantic slope. There were dwarfed and storm-battered trees at timberline with here and there a forest lake or a grassy opening showing down in the woods. There were only a few snowdrifts. Far out to the east about one hundred miles I could see the dry, brown plains in eastern Colorado.

But looking down the slope to the west everything was white. From a few hundred feet below where I was standing and westward for one hundred miles, snow lay deep over everything; forests, mountains, and valleys were all in white. It frequently happens that while one mountainous region is very wintry, another locality on the opposite side of the same mountains may be having mild weather. These conditions are often found along opposite sides of the Continental Divide; occasionally there is a storm on the eastern side and not the western, and sometimes it is cold on the western side while there is warm sunshine on the eastern. But I enjoy all weather.

I stood looking westward at this steep, snowy slope down the very roof of the world. What a place to coast! I at once wished for a dozen other boys to try it with me. This would be the place for speed—steep places with long plunges—great rushes through the air. Hills and special toboggan slides would be gentle and tame compared with this steep, wild mountain side. Wading out into the snow I sat down on my snowshoes and away we went, coasting toward Pacific sea level. Of course I exceeded the speed limit. The smooth slope dropped nearly a thousand feet in a half mile. Toward the bottom I struck the smoothest place of all. Here was a spring that had overflowed before the snow fell and coated the slope with almost smooth ice. Over this icy slope I went like a rocket. Near the bottom it flattened out abruptly and I was shot several feet into the air over a rainbow pathway—like a football kicked for a goal. At the highest point I looked down into the tops of timberline trees.

After twenty or thirty feet through the air I came back to earth and swept forward and downward at a hair-raising pace. One of the dwarfed little trees that barely stuck up through the snow caught into my snowshoe and hung on. The shoe was torn off and left hanging on the tree top, while I tumbled head over heels into four feet of snow. But this was the greatest coast I ever had. I looked back up the slope along the mark I had made. It would be sundown in about two hours, and it would take about that long to climb up to the place where I had started to coast. Rescuing the snowshoe I climbed up the slope and slid off the roof of the world again.

It was dark when this coast ended. Pushing my sleeping bag into a loose snowdrift, I brushed the snow off myself and slipped into the bag, planning after a sleep to get up, make a fire, and have supper—of raisins—but I slept through the night.

It was not yet daylight when I awoke, but I concluded to have another royal coast. I again climbed the slope and down I rushed, landing several hundred feet to the north and a quarter of a mile below my night camp.

After getting my sleeping bag I went on down the slope where I found tracks of many kinds in the deep snow in the forest. There were stitch-like tracks of mice, big tracks of snowshoe rabbits, trails of squirrels to their supplies of winter cones under the snow, and tracks made by grouse, camp birds, and crested jays. I came upon the place where a mouse had peeped out of a hole in the snow and had been captured by an owl. At another place a coyote, after miles of zigzag wandering, had surprised and captured a grouse beneath a snowcovered bush. I crossed the tracks of a three-footed snowshoe rabbit followed by the tracks of a wildcat and wished I knew their story. But at last I came to the tracks of big animals—just what I was looking for.

In snowy regions the moose, deer, and elk have winter ways which enable them to make a living and to outwit their enemies. A number collect in a small area as the snow begins to deepen and keep the snow well trampled down so that they can walk on top of it. Crisscross trails and their connected trampled spaces enable the animals to run about, to retreat, to fight off their enemies, and to find something to eat. In autumn they eat the mosses and dry grass, as the snow deepens the twigs and leaves on the low-growing shrubbery—alder, willow, and birch—and as they trample the deepening snow and still keep on top of it they feed upon the low limbs of the aspen and other trees and spruce and hemlock needles.

I came upon the winter yard of thirty or forty deer—a trampled space of a half mile along the fishhook course of a mountain stream. A stretch of trampled trail passed beneath arching willows. At one point there was a small, wet and spongy area on both sides of the stream where much of the snow had melted as it fell. Over this the deer had repeatedly trampled, eating the leaves and stalks of the blue Mertensia and other plants. These were still green, having been crushed down and preserved beneath the first snowfall.

One steep stretch of the stream was very swift and, together with the trampling in, it had not frozen over. Here in the open water the deer had eaten all of the moss and water plants within reach. Near the point of the "yard" a snow-slide had come down from the long slope above, carrying off nearly all of the snow in its path and clearing a space about two hundred feet wide and several hundred feet long. Over this cleared space the deer had trampled, eating the exposed dead vegetation. In it they had often sunned themselves and lain down.

A deer yard full of animals is not to be seen every day. So I decided not to go farther but to have a look into every corner of this yard, and also to watch these big-eared, whitetailed fellows. If I wanted other excitement there was a deep, dark canyon near by that might be looked into. Near the yard I made a permanent camp. I built a fire in front of a cliff which soon melted the snow and made a little dry open place for my sleeping bag. I usually kept a fire going all night, rising two or three times to put on wood. Before getting into the sleeping bag I took off my shoes and put on a pair of moccasins, leaving all of my other clothes on. The canvas lining of my sleeping bag was removed each day and aired.

I ranged around this deer yard for two days. In walking through and around it I occasionally came close to the deer. They retreated without great alarm, usually over several of the crisscrossing trails, to another part of the yard. Lion tracks leading into the yard from the woods showed that a lion had sneaked upon the deer. But evidently he had been outwitted.

Climbing down into a deep, snowy canyon, a tree limb that I was clinging to broke and I tumbled forward. In falling I had a glimpse of a fresh bear track in the snow where I was to alight. I had been hoping to see a bear track but when I landed upon this one I did not know what to do with it. Quickly scrambling to my feet I looked all around but could see only a few yards off because of thick timber. Suddenly I heard a furry rustle behind. I turned quickly, stepped on a snowshoe, and took another header. A camp bird behind me gave a low call. Then I braced up.

A bear track at any time is exciting enough, but it is a hair-raising surprise to fall upon one in a canyon. From where I stood I could see that this fellow had reared up with forepaws against a tree limb and I suppose looked and listened. Closer to me the mixed-up tracks and a bunch of hair on a limb showed that he had been scratching his back. Moving slowly and softly from tree to tree I slipped forward. The tracks entered a regular trail deep in the snow where this bear had gone back and forth. I followed this, cautiously, to the side of a dark wooden canyon where there was a bear den.

From the den the trail led up the side of a canyon, across a little opening in the forest, and then on top of a large crag. Here in the sunshine the bear could see in all directions. Apparently this bear had come forth from his den a number of times and made his way to this crag to enjoy a sun bath.

Nearly all bears hibernate. Grizzly bears in the Rockies near my home hibernate from three to five months. I have found their dens in the side of a canyon beneath the roots of a tree, beneath a number of fallen logs, or in a little tunnel in a gravelly mountain side; and a few times I have found dens beneath a regular haysack of limbs, trash, grass, and bark which the bear piled up and then crawled into. With his stomach empty, about the first of December, the bear crawls into his den and goes to sleep. He appears not to eat or drink anything until the next spring. But grizzly bears, and perhaps other bears, occasionally come forth toward spring for an airing or for exercise.

I started to return to my camp by the cliff, but on the way I encountered another fresh grizzly bear track. I backtracked this, planning to examine his abandoned den. But it was close to night when I arrived, and as I was several miles from camp I thought to spend the night in the den. The gravelly floor was perfectly clean except for a few bits of dried skin off his feet and some hair, but the den was too smelly. So out I went to spend the night in the open without my sleeping bag. A short distance from the den I found a cave-like place between large rocks. Cutting a number of small tree limbs I stuffed these into the larger openings between rocks and shut off the wind in that direction. Then using a snowshoe I scooped out the snow and started a small fire burning all over the floor of the cave to warm and dry it.

I was in the edge of a forest of fire-killed trees and there was plenty of wood. Although it was rather snowy handling I gathered a quantity. I laid down three short logs in front of the opening, across these I laid smaller ones, and on top of these piled still smaller ones, with kindling at the top.

Pushing the small fire to the front I set fire to this big pile at the top so that it would burn slowly. On the fire-warmed ground I slept three hours with out wakening. Then the fire had pretty well burned down; my thermometer said it was ten below zero. But there was no air stirring and the night was surprisingly calm. Throwing on more wood I had another sleep. On awakening I started to trail the bear.

I did not have a gun, but the wilds are one of the safest places in the world without one. Bears attempt to kill only those who attempt to kill them, and I hadn't any notion of trying this. What I was doing in the way of camping any boy could do, and it wouldn't cost much, either. My equipment was not at all expensive. About all there was to it was the sleeping bag and the snowshoes. Of course I always carried a camera.

Trailing this bear took me within a quarter of a mile of my camp. I got my sleeping bag, thinking to be better prepared for the next night in case I trailed the bear far away. After wandering about in the woods for some miles the bear struck straight for the top of the Continental Divide. At two o'clock in the afternoon I followed his tracks over the top and started down the eastern slope. We then were at least fifteen miles from his former den. On reaching timberline on the eastern side he started along the mountainside as though going to a definite place, so I walked slowly, keeping a sharp lookout for him. At last, looking with my field glass, I saw him sitting in the sunshine by a hole which evidently was the entrance to an old den.

After watching him for some time he rolled over in the snow, rubbed his back, then went into the hole. Apparently he had become tired of his former den or for some other cause had made a change. Probably he had used this second den before.

Although I planned to call on settlers on the western slope, I found that a bear had led me halfway home. I had not seen a single person or passed even a deserted house.

My days for this vacation were numbered as I was now on the eastern side of the Divide, I started homeward over the twenty-mile stretch to my cabin. The coyotes yelped merrily under the stars. I could readily see to travel at night. At about one o'clock in the morning I threw my sleeping bag on the floor of my cabin.

Enos' homestead cabin.

Go to the winter Woods: Listen there, look, watch, and "the dead months" will give you a subtler secret than any you have yet found in the forest.
Fiona Macleod

Winter Ways of Animals

On the way home one winter afternoon I came upon a beaver colony a little below timberline. In the edge of the woods I stood for a time looking out on the white smooth pond. Lines of tracks crossed it from every point of the compass. Two camp birds alighted on a tree within a few feet and looked me over. I heard a flock of chickadees going through the woods.

A lynx came out of the willow clumps on the opposite shore. He walked out on the snowy pond and headed straight for the house. He was in no hurry and stepped slowly along and climbed on top of the house. Here he sniffed a time or two, then raked the house with right forepaw. He sniffed again. Nothing in reach for him.

Climbing down off the beaver house the lynx walked around it and started for the woods near me. Catching my scent he stopped, took a look, then went full speed into the Englemann spruce forest. Other lynx had visited the top of the beaver house and also prowled along the bottom of the dam. A number of mountain sheep had crossed the pond a day or two before.

The pond was in a deep gulch and a goodly stream of water out of sight beneath the ice and snow was running into it. The concentrated outflow burst out over the top of the south end of the dam through an eighteen-inch opening. This pond was frozen over for five months. For these five months the beaver each day had a swim or two in the water under the ice. When hungry he took a section of an aspen from the pile on the bottom of the pond. This was dragged under the ice up into the house, where it afforded a meal of canned green bark.

Most summer birds fly away from winter. Other birds and a few animals travel a short distance—go to a place where food is more abundant although the winter there may not be any milder than in the locality in which they summered. Birds that remain to winter in the locality in which they summered, and most of the animals, too, go about their affairs as usual. They do not store food for the winter or even for the following day. The getting of food in the land of snows does not appear to trouble them.

But a number of animals—squirrels, chipmunks, conies, and beavers—store food for the winter. Generally these supplies are placed where they are at all times readily reached by the owners; on the earth, in it, in the water; the place depending on the taste and the habits of the fellow.

Upon the mountain tops the cony, or Little Chief Hare, stacks hay each autumn. This tiny stack is placed in the shelter of a big boulder or by a big rock, close to the entrance of his den. While the beaver is eating green canned bark the cony is contentedly chewing dry, cured hay.

The beaver is one of the animals which solves the winter food and cold problem by storing a harvest of green aspen, birch, and willow. This is made during the autumn and is stored on the bottom of the pond below the ice-line. Being canned in cold water the bark remains fresh for months.

Squirrel store nuts and cones for winter food. Most squirrels have a regular storing place. This covers only a few square yards or less and usually is within fifty or sixty feet of the base of the tree in which the squirrel has a hole and a winter home.

Commonly, when dining, the squirrel goes to his granary or storage place and uses this for a dining room. A squirrel in a grove near my cabin sat on the same limb during each meal. He would take a cone, climb up to this limb, about six feet above the snow, back up against the tree and began eating. One day an owl flew into the woods. The squirrel dropped his cone and scampered up into the treetop without a chirp.

Another day a coyote came walking through the grove without a sound. He had not seen me and I did not see him until the squirrel suddenly exploded with a sputtering rush of squirrel words. He denounced the coyote, called him a number of names. The coyote did not like it, but what could he do? He took one look at the squirrel and walked on. The squirrel, hanging to the cone in his right hand, waved it about and cussed the coyote as far as he could see him.

A number of species of chipmunks store quantities of food, mostly weed seed. But no one appears to know much of the winter life of chipmunks.

Chipmunks around my home remain under ground more than half of the year. Two near my cabin were out of their holes only four months one year. They were busy these four months gathering seeds and peanuts which they stored underground in their tunnels. Twice by digging I found the chipmunks in a sleep so heavy that I could not awaken them, and I believe they spend much of the eight months underground sleeping. Digging also revealed that they had eaten but little of their stored supplies.

When food becomes scarce and the weather cold and snowy, a number of animals hole up—go into a den. By hibernating, sleeping away the weeks the earth is barren and white, they triumph over the ways of winter. Bears and groundhogs are famous hibernaters. Many chipmunks and some species of squirrels hibernate for indefinite periods.

> The Bat and the Bear, they never care
> What winter winds may blow;
> The Jumping-mouse in his cozy house
> Is safe from ice and snow.
>
> The Chipmunk and the Woodchuck,
> The Skunk, who's slow but sure,
> The ringed Raccoon, who hates the moon,
> Have found for cold the cure.
> —Samuel Scovill, Jr., in Everyday Adventures.

Animals which hibernate, fast and sleep through much or all of the winter, are not harmed and possibly are benefitted by the fasting and sleeping. Bears and groundhogs are fat when they go to bed in the autumn and fat and strong when they come out in the spring.

A snowy winter gives a bear den a cold-excluding outer covering—closes the entrance and the airholes. Most bears and groundhogs appear to remain in the den all winter. I have known an occasional groundhog to thrust out his head for a few minutes now and then during the winter, and bears may come forth and wander about for a time, especially if not quite comfortable. I have known a number of bears to come out toward spring for brief airings and sunnings.

Midwinter a bear wanted more bedding. In fact, he did not have any, which was unusual. But the winter was cold, no snow had fallen, and the frigid wind was whistling through his poorly built den house. The usual snow would have closed the air holes and shut out the cold. He was carrying cedar bark and mouthfuls of dried grass into the den.

This same winter I came upon another bear. Cold or something else had driven him from his den. When I saw him he was trying to reopen an old den which was back in a bank under the roots of a spruce. He may have tried to dig a den elsewhere, but the ground was frozen almost as hard as stone. While he was working a bobcat came snarling out. The bear struck at it. It backed off sputtering then ran away. In tearing out a root the bear slipped and rolled down the bank. He went off through the woods.

Late one February I came upon a well-worn bear trail between the sunny side of a cliff and an open den. In this trail there were tracks fresh and tracks two or more weeks old. Elsewhere I have seen many evidences that bears toward spring come out briefly to sun themselves and to have an airing. But never a sign of their eating or drinking anything.

Near my cabin I marked four groundhog holes after the fat fellows went in. On September tenth I stuffed a bundle of grass in the entrance of each den. Sometime during the winter one of them had disturbed the grass and thrust out his head. Whether this was on Groundhog Day or not, I cannot say. The other groundhogs remained below until between April seventh and twelfth, about seven months. And these seven months were months of fast, and possibly without water.

The raccoon, who ever seems a bright, original fellow, appears to have a hibernating system of his own. Many a raccoon takes a series of short hibernating sleeps each winter, and between these sleeps he is about hunting food, eating and living as usual. But I believe these periods of hibernating often correspond to stormy or snowy periods.

While trying to see a flock of wild turkeys in Missouri one winter day I had a surprise. The snow showed that they had come out of the woods and eaten corn from a corn shock. I hoped to see them by using a nearby shock for a blind and walked around the shock. The snow over and around it showed only an outgoing mouse track. No snow had fallen for two days.

I had gotten into the center of the shock when I stepped on something that felt like a big dog. But a few seconds later, when it lunged against me, trying blindly to get out, it felt as big as a bear. I overturned the shock in escaping. A blinking raccoon looked at me for a few seconds, then took to the woods.

Deep snow rarely troubles wild life who lay up food for winter. And snow sometimes is even helpful to food storers and also to the bears and groundhogs who hibernate, and even to a number of small folk who neither hibernate nor lay up supplies.

One winter afternoon I followed down the brook which flows past my cabin. The last wind had blown from an unusual quarter, the northeast. It made haystack drifts in a number of small aspen groves. One of these drifts was perhaps twenty feet across and about as high. The treetops were sticking out of it.

On the top of the snowdrift a cottontail was feeding happily off the bark of the small limbs. This raised platform had given him a good opportunity to get at a convenient food supply. He was making the most of this. At the bottom he had bored a hole in the snow pile and apparently planned to live there.

While peeping into this hole two mice scampered along it. This snow would protect them against coyotes. Safe under the snow they could make their little tunnels, eat grass and gnaw bark, without the fear of a coyote jumping upon them.

Tracks and records in the snow showed that for two days a coyote did not capture a thing to eat. During this time he had traveled miles. He had closely covered a territory about three miles in diameter. There was game in it, but his luck was against him. He was close to a rabbit, grabbed a mouthful of feathers—but the grouse escaped, and even looked at a number of deer. At last, after more than two days, and possibly longer, he caught a mouse or two.

Antelope in the plains appear to live in the same territory the year round. Many times in winter I have been out on the plains and found a flock feeding where I had seen it in summer. But one snowy time they were gone. I found them about fifteen miles to the west, where either less snow had fallen or the wind had partly swept it away. The antelope were in good condition. While I watched them a number started a race.

The wolves had also moved. A number of these big gray fellows were near the antelope. Just what the other antelope and the other wolves who used this locality did about these new, folks, I cannot guess.

Mountain deer and elk who usually range high during the summer go to the lowlands or several miles down the mountains for the winter. They may thus be said to migrate vertically. One thousand feet of descent equals, approximately, the climatic changes of a thousand-mile southward journey. They may thus winter from five to twenty-five miles from where they summered, from one thousand to several thousand feet lower. The elk that winter in the Jackson Hole region have a summer range on the mountains forty or fifty miles away. But elk and deer that have a home territory in the lowlands are likely to be found summer after summer in the same small, unfenced pasture.

Moose, caribou, deer, and elk during heavy snows often resort to yarding. Moose and caribou are experts in taking care of themselves during long winters of deep snow. They select a yard which offers the maximum food supply and other winter opportunities.

One snowy winter I visited a number of elk that were yarding. High peaks rose snowy and treeless above the home in the forest. The ragged-edged yard was about half a mile long and a quarter of a mile wide. About one half the yard was a swamp covered with birch and willow and a scattering of fir. The remainder was a combination of open spaces, aspen groves, and a thick growth of spruce.

Constant trampling compressed the snow and enabled the elk readily to move about. Outside the yard they would bogged in deep snow. In the swamp the elk reached the moss, weeds, and other growths. But toward spring the grass and weeds had either been eaten or were buried beneath icy snow. The elk then ate aspen twigs and the tops and limbs and bark of birch and willow.

Ease of movement in this area enabled the elk to keep enemies at bay. Several times I saw from tracks that lion had entered this self-made wild life reservation, and on two occasions a number of wolves invaded it. Each time the elk had bunched in a pocket of a trampled space and effectively fought off the wolves.

One day late in February I visited the yard. The elk plainly had lost weight but were not in bad condition. While I lingered near the entire herd joined merrily in chase and tag, often racing then wheeling to rear high and fence with heads. If I counted correctly this herd went through the entire winter without the loss of an elk.

The caribou appears to be the only animal which migrates between summer and winter ranges, that is, which makes a long journey of hundreds of miles; as much change of place as made by many species of migrating birds. The main cause for this migration is the food supply, but myriads of mosquitoes in the woods may be one cause of the moose moving each summer far into the north where there are grassy prairies and large openings in the woods. But for winter they seek food and shelter in a yard in the forest.

While snowshoeing in the forested mountains to the southeast of Long's Peak I came upon a mountain lion track startlingly fresh. I followed it to a den beneath a rock pile at the bottom of a cliff. Evidently the lion was in. Seeing older tracks which he had made on leaving the den, I trailed these. After zigzagging through the woods he had set off in a beeline for the top of a cliff. From this point he evidently saw a number of deer. He had crawled forward, then backtracked and turned to the right, then made round to the left. The snow was somewhat packed and his big feet held him on the surface. The deer broke through.

The lion climbed upon a fallen tree and crept forward. He was screened by its large upturned root. At last he rushed out and seized a nearby deer and killed it, evidently after a short struggle. He had then pursued and killed a young deer that fled off to the left where it was struggling in the heavy snows. Without returning to the first kill the lion fed off the second and returned to the den.

I followed the other deer. In a swamp they had fed for a time on the tops of tall weeds among the snow and willows. I came close to them in a thick growth of spruce. Here the snow was less deep. A goodly portion of the snow still clung to the trees.

These deer circled out of the spruce swamp and came into their trail made in entering it. Back along this trail they followed to where the lion had made the first kill. Leaping over this dead deer they climbed up on the rocky ridge off which so much snow had blown that they could travel speedily most of the time over the rocks with only now and then a stretch of deep snow.

Often during my winter trips I came upon a porcupine. Both winter and summer he seemed blindly content. There were ten thousand trees around, and winter or summer there were meals to last a lifetime. Always he had a dull, sleepy look and I doubt if he ever gets enthusiastic enough to play.

Birds that remain all winter in snowy lands enjoy themselves. Like the winter animals, usually they are well fed. But most species of birds with their airplane wings fly up and down the earth, go northward in the spring and southward in the autumn, and thus linger where summer lingers and move with it when it moves.

Around me the skunks hibernated about two months each year; some winters possibly not at all. Generally the entire skunk family, from two to eight, hole up together. One den which I looked into in midwinter had a stack of eight sleepy skunks in it. A bank had caved off exposing them. I left them to sleep on, for had I wakened them they might not have liked it. And who wants to mix up with a skunk?

Another time a snowslide tore a big stump out by the roots and disclosed four skunks beneath. When I arrived, about half an hour after the tear-up, the skunks were blinking and squirming as though apparently too drowsy to decide whether to get up or to have another good sleep.

Many tales have been told about the terrible hunger and ferocity of wolves during the winter. This may sometimes be so. Wolves seem ever to have good, though not enormous, appetites. Sometimes, too, they go hungry for days without a full meal. But generally, if the winter is snowy, this snow makes it easier for them to make a big kill.

Deer, elk, and mountain sheep occasionally are caught in deep snow, or are struck by a snowslide. A number sometimes are snowbound or killed at one time. Usually the prowling wolves or coyotes discover the kill and remain near as long as the feast holds out.

Once I knew of a number of wolves and two lions lingering for more than two weeks at the wreckage brought down by a snowslide. I was camping down below in the woods and each evening heard a hullabaloo, and when awake in the night I heard it. Occasionally I heard it in the daytime. Finally a grizzly made a discovery of this feeding ground. He may have scented it or he may have heard the uproars a mile or two away. For the wolves and the lions feasted, fought, and played by the hour. The row became so uproarious one night that I started up to see what it was all about. But the night was dark and I turned back to wait until morning. Things had then calmed down, and only the grizzly remained. After he ran off I found that from fifteen to twenty deer had been swept down by the slide and mixed with the tree wreckage.

The right kind of winter clothing is an important factor for winter life for both people and animals. The clothing problem perhaps is more important than the food question.

Winter in the Temperate Zone causes most birds and animals to change clothing—to put on a different suit. This usually is of winter weight and in many cases of a different color than that of the summer suit. Bears, beavers, wolves, and sheep put on a new, bright, heavy suit in autumn and by spring this is worn and faded. The weasel wears yellow-brown clothes during summer, but during winter is in pure white fur—the tip of the tail only being jet black. The snowshoe rabbit has a new suit at the beginning of each winter. This is a furry, warm, and pure white. His summer clothes are a trifle darker in color than those of other rabbits. If there is no snow he eats with his feet on the earth or on a fallen log or rock pile, but if there is a deep snow he has snowshoes fastened on and is ever ready to go lightly over the softest surface.

In these ways—hibernating, eating stored food, or living as in summer time from hand to mouth—the animals of the Temperate Zone go contentedly through the winter with a change of habit and all with a change of clothing. The winter commonly is without hardship and there is time for pranks and play. Winter, so the animal Eskimos say, and so the life of the Temperate Zone shows, will bear acquaintance.

A frozen-over beaver pond,
Twin Sisters Mountain in the background.

Passion remakes the world.
Ralph Waldo Emerson

Snowslides from Start to Finish

One snowy March evening I arrived on web snowshoes at a miners' boarding house high up in the Twelve Mile range of mountains where snowslides are common in spring. I had come to see snowslides, and after I had spent all evening hearing the miners tell about them I was more anxious than ever to see how snowslides "run."

Next morning I was up early and all ready when the foreman came out and asked, "Has the Ferguson run yet? Well, then, tell Sullivan to start her." Looking in my direction, he added, "Tell him to take this fellow along."

I followed Sullivan's example and seized a ten pound rock fragment on the dump, then hurried along, trying on web shoes to keep up with Sullivan's long skee strides.

"The Ferguson," I learned, as we hustled along, was the name of a gulch; and the thing the foreman wanted started was the snow in the upper end. Several times each winter, as soon as snow from storm or wind accumulated in the gulch or on the summit rim, the snow ran out in a slide—the Ferguson slide. When it failed to start promptly of its own accord after a heavy snowstorm the miners started it. It was dangerous to use the road over the gulch, half a mile below, with the snowslide impending. A slide of several hundred tons of snow could rush the full length of the smooth, steep-sided gulch in a minute or less, although it was from a quarter to half a mile deep and more than a mile long.

The mine building stood on the top of the plateau a short distance from the head of the gulch. Whirling winds made a current down the gulch, but as they swept over the rim the current was broken and much of the wind-carried snow was dropped, forming in a few hours an enormous snow cornice at the upper rim of the gulch. Here we stopped.

"Throw her there," directed Sullivan.

My ten pound rock made a snowy splash. Instantly a wagonload of snow slipped, then the entire cornice caved off and the whole mass of

Long's Peak from the north,
Rocky Mountain National Park.

snow in the upper end of the gulch started sliding. With a rush and roar it swept down the gulch. Whirling, back-flying snow filled the sky above the canyon with snowflakes and snow dust. The Ferguson had run.

I climbed down the cleaned-out gulch and hurried eagerly to have a look at the snow that had just run—the dead slide—but it took me nearly half an hour to traverse the distance which the slide by actual timing had made in fifty-two seconds. Occasionally, when there is more snow, the Ferguson slide coasts even farther than this one did, sometimes a quarter of a mile.

The big, white dump was spread out over a level flat and covered a space about three times the size of a baseball diamond, four feet deep in places. A part of the snow was jammed into big, icy snowballs, chunks as big as a barrel, but most of it looked like coarse white sand. The Ferguson ran so often that it kept the gulch well cleaned, and there was but little trash or gravel in the snow.

One windy day I came to a fresh snowslide dump where slides had run down three gulches that joined in a canyon and piled their snow and dirt in one huge heap to the depth of nearly one hundred feet. A wagon road was buried. But a tunnel had just been opened through this snowy blockade. Remains of this well packed snow were still there the fourth of the following July.

Another day I climbed high up on the slopes of a peak, now called Mount Guyot I think, surrounded by canyons and steep, long slopes without number. Clinging to the sides of one of the sharp ridges that jutted out from the plateau below were enormous snow cornices, drifted and formed by the winter winds. I saw several slides make rushing coasts, stirring up white dust and filling the air with crashing which the echoing mountain walls multiplied into riots.

Several times a slide in running dislodged rock piles or snow piles and these in turn developed other slides, marking a tremendous, confusing uproar. An airplane in the sky above might have had a show of gigantic snowy rockets and meteors as the slides rushed down this slope and that, exploding here and there in dust columns as cliffs and walls were struck.

Head-on a slide ran into a canyon wall. The pressure and violence of striking had changed—frozen—the snow to ice. For more than one hundred and fifty feet up on the wall, ice, snow, and broken trees were frozen fast.

About noon a large snow cornice fell away and shot down the slope carrying numbers of snowdrifts along with it. After a long run it shot up the slope opposite, struck a big circular basin, circled, and finally slid down the wall of this back into its own track where it started up the slope. It had run a loop.

In the midst of an uproar I could hear crashes and booming from the slope opposite me. This steep slope was against a high plateau that faced me and above this a precipitous walled peak stood up in the sky far above the timberline.

In rushing forward to see it I narrowly missed running in front of a monstrous breaker of a slide that was rushing up the slope. Rocks, dirty snow, and broken trees were tumbling in its front. Several broken trees stuck forward from its front at a dangerous angle: two of these dropped into the snow in front and were explosively torn out and crushed beneath the rushing mass.

This slide was a ponderous and chaotic affair. It had started on the peak opposite and about two thousand feet higher than where it nearly caught me. Down more than a mile of steep slope it had smashed its way, bringing trash, snow, and hundreds of trees with it. It must have been moving at high speed when it reached the bottom, and it was not in low gear when it passed me. And I was a quarter of a mile above the bottom.

On it rushed—still full of mountain momentum. Less than two hundred feet up the slope it rushed over the top of a ridge, rammed a gigantic snow cornice, filled the air with flying snow masses, and disappeared over the top in a whirling cloud of snowy white. By the time I reached the top it was tearing down the slope half a mile below, completely concealed behind an enormous screen of snow dust.

In the spring one cannot be certain where or when a slide will start. Big canyons are joined by several smaller canyons. A slide may run down one of these smaller canyons any hour. But all these slides run through the big canyon. I had just crossed a big canyon when three slides, each from a smaller canyon, rushed by like snow express trains.

Although slides run wild and simply refuse to be stopped until the coast is ended, they can be anchored or fastened so that they will not start. In numerous canyons and on most slopes the snow will not slip and

A man takes his horses across a snowfield.

slide unless hit by rocks or snow from overladen steeps above. Many mountain villages or mine buildings are effectively protected by anchoring the snow deposit which starts a slide and makes the trouble. I have seen slides corralled in this way—hogtied as it were—so they could not start.

One mine which I visited was on a steep slope above the treeline and not far from the top of the mountains where winds blew deep drifts. Twice these snowdrifts had slipped, and the huge slides had swept down upon the buildings and carried them, smashed, to the bottom of the canyon a mile below. But for several years these snowdrifts had not slid, for they were securely anchored by four rows of stout posts across the slopes where snow accumulated. Sometimes stone walls are used for the purpose. The snow settles over, hangs on, is held fast.

At another place a slide came down a few times each winter between the two main buildings of a mine. As no effective way had been found to anchor the snow two men were placed on lookout after each snowstorm to fire warning shots the instant the slide started.

A slide may usually be heard. It roars or rushes crashing. But down in the bottom of a canyon where one cannot see far ahead the echoes stirred by a slide are confusing. Mountain walls echo and reecho; canyons commonly are crooked; it ofttimes is difficult to determine the direction from which a slide is approaching. Being run down by a slide usually means death, but the number of slides in any snowy locality is not numerous and the number of people annually killed and injured by them commonly is fewer than a week's auto injuries in New York City.

Ice and snow in any form ever are slippery. Snowslides are brought about by heavy falls of snow on steep, smooth slopes, and by winds which sweep the snow off wide areas and drop it in drifts at the tops of slopes. A snowslide could never occur in a level country no matter how much snow accumulated. I did, however, see a small, lively snowslide rush off a big, steep barn roof, creating much excitement among us boys who were making a snow elephant a few feet away.

Probably more slides move during March than in other month. Roughly, there are three kinds of slides, or rather, three sets of conditions that start slides. Slides that start during or shortly after a snowfall from the steep walls or slopes of canyons commonly follow the long used channels made by streams or snowslides. These same channels may often be used by the slide that takes all winter to form. A part of each winter snowfall is drifted at the top of a mountain and after weeks a large drift results. There is a breaking up during the spring thaw in March and the winter's accumulation of snow slips and slides away. The third type of slide comes down over rough places where a slide has not before coasted. A slide of this kind may be formed by a wind from an unusual quarter drifting the snow heavily in a place where snow does not ordinarily drift; or through several years' accumulation of snow and ice, winter after winter the pile grows larger and at last tips over, or its foundation —through much freezing and thawing—gives way.

Once a slide starts there seems to be no stopping it. It usually goes straight for the bottom and one can see its long, gouged opening from starting to stopping place. But not always. A slide in a crooked canyon winds like a stream. Often if one starts down a fishhook-bent gulch it will follow the bends. But it may jump over a low wall; and, occasionally, when a slide is speeding down a crooked gulch, it jumps out.

I was one day walking serenely along the top of a canyon when a slide in the canyon concluded to jump out. Wildly rumbling and roaring, a mass of snow and snow-dust suddenly shot up and out at me. In the cloud of snow-dust I lost sight of everything. Then came a rush of wind, and through the cleared air I saw the slide turn a somersault out of a canyon and land on its back on the wall opposite. For half a minute or longer a great white column of smoke screen snow-powder and snow-dust filled the canyon and rose higher and higher until it was perhaps a quarter of a mile high. In rushing down the canyon and in ramming the wall, tons of snow and ice had been crushed to powder and this caught up by the excited air had made a strange, grand display. I had seen slides do high-jumping, dive over canyons, sideswipe a wall and tip bottom side up, but this somersaulting was a new stunt for slides.

Well up the slope above Hoosier Pass I found an old snowdrift which had lain for years. It was more like ice than snow. But there was not enough ice to make a glacier nor was the rough wooded slope steep enough for the ice and snow to slide and run down. So there it lay, lasting through many summers and getting larger each year. It must have weighed a few thousand tons. It was topheavy and leaning forward. If it fell to the east, down a slope it would go; if it tumbled to the north, it would plunge down a gully, then down a slope. But whichever way it went a little more of spring warmth and its icy moorings would release it. A stream of water from a spring thaw on a warm slope was undermining one corner.

In crossing a canyon to the cabin of a prospector I looked back over my shoulder to see that it was not starting as I began to descend the slope. But the cabin which stood a stone's throw from the bottom of the gully seemed safe from snowslides.

In the little log cabin the prospector and I had a happy evening. We sat late by the sheet-iron stove while I listened to his experiences with bears, Indians, and snowslides. In Idaho he had worked two years driving a tunnel into a mountainside. All the wood burned during this time was from a mass of forest wreckage brought down by a slide. So big was the pile that all he used made but little showing on it.

"Yes," he said, "the slide is likely to break loose any hour. It will smash through several stretches of forest in going down the mile or more of steep slope to the bottom of the canyon. There will be a vast pile of broken timber, rocks large and small, and quantities of dirty snow and ice in one big mass together. But I think the cabin is secure from slides, although the big snow- and icefield when it runs will come close to it."

The next morning I climbed into the heights while the prospector climbed down a short distance to work in a tunnel. Thinking to see the big old ice- and snow-field if it started to run I kept in sight of it most of the day. But it did not move, although others had moved or were moving. I saw a path where a number of slides had run; two had jumped over high cliffs. I heard others running in deep canyons where I could not see them, but the steamy clouds of white ice- and snow-powder which rolled up out of the canyon behind them were a wonder show. Often one can see this back streamer of snow-dust from a canyon when the slide itself is too far away to be heard or seen.

I found a slope where two slides had collided. One had slid for half a mile down a smooth slope and developed speed enough to carry it far up the opposite slope when it met another slide speeding down. For two hundred feet around the snow was splashed with slide wreckage; broken trees, rocks, and ice had torn up the snow and plastered the trees on the side lines. It was a head-on collision. But one side of the slide coming down turned in after the crash and kept on going. After a few hundred feet it jumped over a cliff and wrecked a grove in the canyon.

On the way home I had a surprise, for I did not expect to be taken as a passenger on a slide. While I was snowshoeing down a smooth, steep mountain side the snow suddenly skinned off and slid, and my feet were knocked from under me. It was fortunate I soon reached some trees strong enough not to break from the shock, as some did, for my slide was just beginning to get into high speed when I was spilled off, breathless, with my clothes torn, portions of the slide jammed in my neck, and one snowshoe and my hat missing. The snowshoe I found hours later in the snow against a tree stump, but not my hat. I reached the prospector's cabin at midnight.

About ten o'clock the following morning, while I was repairing clothes and snowshoes, there came a crash and roar as though a dozen slides were running at once. Surely the old snow- and ice-field had slipped at last, and I would see it run.

I made a dash for the top of the woodpile. On the way an enormous rock, frozen to a mass of ice, ripped through the air and smashed off a big spruce just beyond the cabin. Had it struck the cabin only scattered kindling wood have remained.

Then came a rush of wind which knocked me off the woodpile. The slide was upon me. Chunks of snow fell about and a wildly whirling cloud of snowdust hid everything. I clapped a handkerchief over my noise to avoid smothering. There were rushing, rumbling, roaring, and trembling. A crash, and in the snow-filled air I saw the flying logs of the cabin. A gust of wind cleared the air as the tail end of the slide went by. Full speed I ran after it; the way was cleared of snow, but I was distanced in a flash.

The mountain side beyond the canyon commenced to boom, crash, and roar with echoes thick and fast, telling of the stir and intensity of the slide, which was dashing through slide rock, smashing through the woods, ramming cliffs, exploding as it went but never stopping, and giving off enough snow-dust for a windstorm.

Yes, the old snow- and ice-field had tipped over and come down to the cabin. The mere edge of the mass had hit the cabin. There must have been four or five thousand tons of snow, ice, gravel, and rocks in the mass that started. But this was small compared with the quantity that reached the bottom of the canyon. Something was added to the slide every foot of the way. There were quantities of snow, rock piles, trainloads of gravel, huge rock fragments from cliffs, and several thousand forest trees.

A squirrel who had had his winter store of cones carried away and who evidently had narrowly escaped being caught, was greatly peeved with this performance. He chattered and scolded. As I came running along, his peppery temper was at its worst and he seemed to be denouncing all snowslides and everything in general.

At the bottom of a steep stretch the slide had smashed through a forest, uprooting or smashing off trees and making an opening thirty-four steps wide. At one place it had leaped and mowed off the trees several feet above the earth. Then mystery! Four trees in a line were left standing, though one of these was skinned of a quantity of its bark.

The ground beneath the slide had been swept bare; grass, trash, loose rocks, and snow were cleaned off and carried away. The four-foot snow cover in the woods on the side lines was splashed and covered with trash and earthy, black snow. Many trees on the slide's edges were barked and numbers were leaning forward. Most limbs were torn off from thirty to fifty feet above the earth. So I suppose the slide had been about thirty feet deep. Jamming in places had caused it to deepen or to throw up ice, rocks, or tree trunks into the air; these would smash things far above the top of the rushing slide.

The thing must have been several hundred feet long. Its wreckage at the bottom contained firewood enough to supply a village for a year. The cabin was in the vast mass of wreckage thrown together in fierce confusion in the bottom of the canyon; also the prospector's winter supplies and my snowshoes. But I had seen a big slide run.

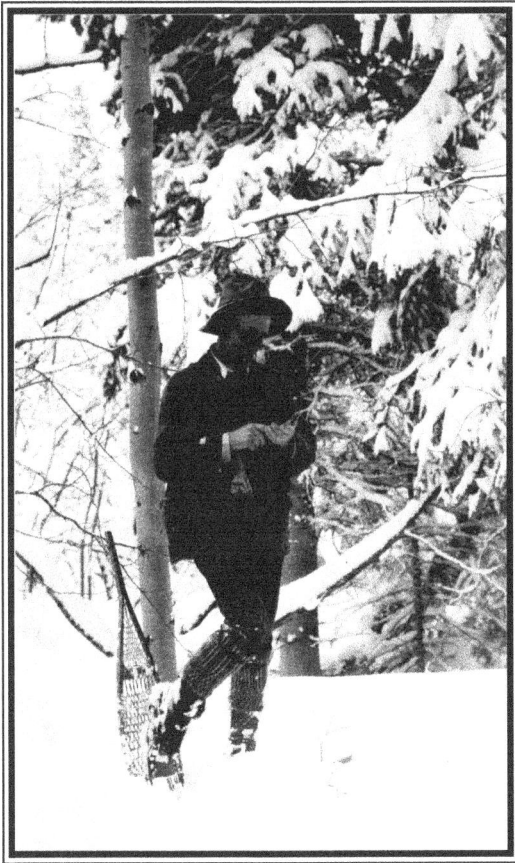

Enos takes a brief rest while snowshoeing.

Out of the bosom of the air
Out of the cloud-folds of her garment shaken.
Over the woodlands brown and bare.
Over the harvest-fields forsaken.
Silent, and soft, and slow
Descends the snow.
　　　Henry Wadsworth Longfellow

In the Winter Snows

For years I wondered how big game managed to live through the hard winters. How did they obtain food while the snows lay deep? Two winters of snowshoeing through the Rocky Mountains as Snow Observer often brought me in contact with wild game. These wanderings, together with numerous winter camping excursions through the woods in other scenes, gave me many a glimpse of the winter manner and customs of big wild folk.

One autumn a heavy snowstorm caught me in the mountains of Colorado without snowshoes. In getting out of this I found it easier to wade down a shallow unfrozen stream than to wallow through deep snow. Presently I came upon a herd of deer who were also avoiding the deep snow by using a waterway. They were traveling along in the river and occasionally paused to feed off the banks. Out all floundered into the snow to let me pass. They reentered the water before I was out of sight.

A few days later I returned on snowshoes to see how they were faring. Deep snow had not seriously concerned them. They were in a snowless place near the river. During the storm an accumulation of sludgy, floating snow had formed a temporary dam in the stream, which raised the water and flooded a nearby flat. Presently the dam went out, and the water ran off; but the water carried with it some of the snow, and it had dissolved much of the remainder. In this cleared place the deer were feeding and loitering.

Wild life easily stands an ordinary storm and usually manages to survive even a deep, long-lying snow. The ability of big game to endure storms must in part be due to their acquaintance with every opportunity

A glacial cirque high in the mountains.

Hikers explore the edges of a high mountain
pond carved by glaciation.

afforded by the restricted district in which they live. Big wild folk do not range afar nor at random, nor do they drift about like gypsies. Most animals range in a small locality,—spend their lives in a comparatively small territory. They are familiar with a small district and thus are able to use it at all times to the best advantage. They know where to find the earliest grass; where flies are least troublesome; the route over which to retreat in case of attack; and where is the best shelter from the storm.

With the coming of a snowstorm big game commonly move to the most sheltered spot in their district. This may or may not be close to a food supply. A usual place of refuge is in a cover or sheltered spot on a sunny southern slope,—a place, too, in which the snow will first melt. Immediately after a storm there may often be found a motley collection of local wild folk in a place of this kind. Bunched, the big game hope and wait. Unless the snow is extremely deep they become restless and begin to scatter after two or three days.

There are a number of places in each locality which may offer temporary, or even permanent, relief to snow-hampered game. These are open streams, flood-cleared flats, open spots around springs, wind-cleared places, and openings, large and small, made by snow-slides. During long-lying deep snows the big game generally use every local spot or opening of vantage.

In many regions a fall of snow is followed by days of fair weather. During these days most of the snow melts; often the earth is almost free of one snow before another fall comes. In places of this kind the game have periods of ease. But in vast territories the snow comes, deepens, and lies deep over the earth for weeks. To endure long-lying deep snows requires special habits or methods. The yarding habit, more or less intensely developed, is common with sheep, elk, deer, and moose of all snowy lands.

The careful yarding habit of the moose is an excellent method of triumphing over deep snow. In early winter, or with the deepening snow, a moose family proceed to a locality where food is abundant; here they restrict themselves to a small stamping ground,—one of a stone's throw or a few hundred feet radius. Constant tramping and feeding in this limited area compacts the snow in spaces and in all the trails so that the animals walk on top of it. Each additional snow is in turn trampled to sustaining compactness.

At first the low growing herbage is eaten; but when this is buried, and the animals are raised up by added snow, they feed upon shrubs; then on the willow or the birch tops, and sometimes on limbs well up in the trees, which the platform of deeply accumulated snow enables them to reach. Commonly moose stay all winter in one yard. Sometimes the giving out of the food supply may drive them forth. Then they try to reach another yard, but deep snow or wolves may overcome one or all on the way.

During one snowshoe trip through western Colorado I visited seven deer yards. One of these had been attacked by wolves but probably without result. Apparently five of the others had not as yet been visited by deadly enemies. The seventh and most interesting yard was situated in a deep gorge amid rugged mountains. It was long and narrow, and in it the deer had fed upon withered grass, plant stalks, and willow twigs. All around the undrifted snow lay deep. The limbless bases of the spruces were set deep in snow, and their lower limbs were pulled down and tangled in it. These trees had the appearance of having been pushed part way up through the snow. In places the cliffs showed their bare brown sides. Entire spruce groves had been tilted to sharp angles by the slipping and dragging snow weight on steep places; among them were tall spruces that appeared like great feathered arrows that had been shot into snowy steeps. The leafless aspens attractively displayed their white and greenish-white skin on limbs that were held just above the snow.

With a curve, the yard shaped itself to the buried stream. It lay between forested and moderately steep mountains that rose high. In this primeval winter scene the deer had faced the slowgoing snow in the primitive way. At the upper end of the yard all the snow was trampled to compactness, and over this animals could walk without sinking in. Firm, too, were the surfaces of the much looped and oft trodden trails. The trail nearest to the stream passed beneath a number of beautiful snow-piled arches. These arches were formed of outreaching and interlacing arms of parallel growths of willow and birch clusters. The stream gurgled beneath its storm window of rough ice.

I rounded the yard and at the lower end I found the carcasses of the entire herd of deer,—nine in all,—evidently recently killed by a mountain lion. He had eaten but little of their flesh. Wolves had not yet discovered this feast, but a number of Rocky Mountain jays were there. The dark spruces stood waiting! No air stirred. Bright sunlight and bluish pine shadows rested upon the glazed whiteness of the snow. The flock of cheerful chickadees feeding through the trees knew no tragedy.

The winter food of big game consists of dead grass, shrubs, twigs, buds and bark of trees, moss, and dry plants. At times grass dries or cures before the frost comes. When thus cured it retains much nutrition,—is, in fact, unraked hay. If blighted by frost it loses its flavor and most of its food value.

During summer both elk and deer range high on the mountain. With the coming of winter they descend to the foothill region, where the elk collect in large herds, living in yards in case of prolonged deep snow. Deer roam in small herds. Occasionally a herd of the older elk will for weeks live in the comparatively deep snow on northern slopes,—slopes where the snow crusts least. Here they browse off alder and even aspen bark.

The present congestion of elk in Jackson Hole represents an abnormal condition brought about by man. The winter feed on which they formerly lived is devoured by sheep or cattle during the summer; a part of their former winter range is mowed for hay; they are hampered by fences. As a result of these conditions many suffer and not a few starve.

Wolves are now afflicting both wild and tame herds in Jackson Hole. Apparently the wolves, which formerly were unknown here in winter, have been drawn thither by the food supply which weak or dead elk afford.

The regular winter home of wild sheep is among the peaks above the limits of tree growth. Unlike elk and deer, the mountain sheep is found in the heights the year round. He may, both in winter and summer, make excursions into the lowlands, but during snowy times he clings to the heights. Here he usually finds a tableland or a ridge that has been freed of snow by the winds. In these snow-free places he can feed and loiter and sometimes look down on unfortunate snowbound deer and elk.

The bunching habit of big game during periods of extreme cold or deep snow probably confers many benefits. It discourages the attacks of carnivorous enemies, and usually renders such attacks ineffective. Crowding also gives the greatest warmth with the least burning of fat fuel. The conservation of energy by stormbound animals is of the utmost importance. Cold and snow make complicated endurance tests; the animals must with such handicaps withstand enemies and sometimes live for days with but little or nothing to eat.

Big game, on occasions, suffer bitterly through a combination of misfortunes. Something may prevent a herd reaching its best shelter, and it must then endure the storm in poor quarters; pursuit may scatter and leave each one stranded alone in a bad place; in such case each will suffer from lonesomeness, even though it endure the cold and defy enemies. Most animals, even those that are normally solitary, appear to want society during emergencies.

A deep snow is sometimes followed by a brief thaw, then by days of extreme cold. The snow crusts, making it almost impossible for big game to move, but encouragingly easy for wolves to travel and to attack. Of course, long periods separate these extremely deadly combinations. Probably the ordinary loss of big game from wolves and mountain lions is less than is imagined.

Some years ago an old Ute Indian told me that during a winter of his boyhood the snow for weeks lay "four ponies deep" over the Rocky Mountains, and that "most elk die, many ponies die, wolves die, and Indian nearly die too." A "Great Snow" of this kind is terrible for wild folk.

Snow and cold sometimes combine to do their worst. The snow covers everything deeply; then follows an unbroken period of extreme cold; the Ice King is again enthroned; the snow fiendishly refuses to melt, and lies for weeks; the endurance of most wild folk becomes exhausted, and birds, herds, and wolves perish. Similar calamities used occasionally to afflict our primitive ancestors.

Over the vast Northwest a feature of the climate is the winter-annihilating Chinook wind. This occasionally saves the people of the wilds when other relief is impossible. The snowy earth is quickly transformed by this warm, dry wind. In a few hours conditions become summer-like. Fortunately, the Chinook often follows a blizzard. Many a time at the eleventh hour it has dramatically saved the waiting, suffering birds and rescued the snow-buried and starving folk of the wilds.

The beaver and the bear are often benefitted by the deep snows which afflict their wild neighbors. During the prolonged hibernating sleep, the bear does not eat, but he commonly needs a thick snowy blanket to keep him comfortable. The beaver has his winter stores on the bottom of the pond beneath the ice. These he reaches from his house by swimming beneath the ice from the house to the food pile. If the ice is not covered by snow, it may, during a cold winter, freeze thickly, even to the bottom, and thus cause a starving time in the beaver colony.

Deep snow appears not to trouble the "stupidest animal in the woods," the porcupine. A deeper snow is for him a higher platform from which the bark on the tree may be devoured. Rabbits, too, appear to fare well during deep snow. This uplift allows them a long feast among the crowded, bud-fruited bush-tops at which they have so often looked in vain.

The chipmunk is not concerned with groundhog day. Last summer he filled his underground granaries with nuts and seeds, and subways connect his underground winter quarters with these stores. But heavy snows, with their excess of water, flood him out of winter quarters in spring earlier than he planned.

One March at the close of a wet snowfall I went out into a nearby pine grove to see the squirrels. One descended from a high hole to the snow and without trouble located and bored down through the snow to his cone deposit. With difficulty he climbed up through the heavy snow with a cone. He did not enjoy floundering through the clinging snow to the tree trunk. At last up he started with a snow-laden cone, in search of a dry seat on which to eat. After climbing a few feet he tumbled back into the unpleasant snow. In some manner the wet snow on the tree trunk had caused his downfall. With temper peppery he gathered himself up, and for a moment glared at me as though about to blame me for his troubles. Then, muttering, he climbed up the tree. Sometimes the chipmunk, and the squirrel also, indulge in hibernating periods of sleep despite their ample stores of convenient food.

The ptarmigan is preeminently the bird of the snows; it is the Eskimo of the bird world. It resides in the land realm of the Farthest North and also throughout the West upon high mountaintops. In the heights it lives above the limits of tree growth, close to snowdrifts that never melt, and in places above the altitude of twelve thousand feet. It is a permanent resident of the heights, and apparently only starvation will drive it to the lowlands. Its winter food consists of seeds of alpine plants and the buds of dwarf arctic willow. This willow is matted, dwarfed, and low growing. When drifted over, the ptarmigan burrow into the snow and find shelter beneath its flattened growth. Here they are in reach of willow buds.

Buds are freely eaten by many kinds of birds; they are the staff of life of the ptarmigan and often of the grouse. They are sought by rabbits and go in with the browse eaten by big game. Buds of trees and shrubs are a kind of fruit, a concentrated food, much of the nature of nuts or tubers.

The cheerful water ouzel, even during the winter, obtains much of its food from the bottom of brooks and lakes. The ouzel spends many winter nights in nooks and niches in the bank between the ice and the water. This is a strange place, though one comparatively safe and sheltered. In getting into the water beneath the ice, the ouzel commonly finds opportunity at the outlet or the inlet of the lake; sometimes through an opening maintained by spring water. There are usually many entrances into the waters of a frozen brook,—openings by cascades and the holes that commonly remain in the ice over swift waters. Excessive snow or extreme cold may close all entrances and thus exclude the ouzel from both food and water. Down the mountain or southward the ouzel then goes.

Woodpeckers and chickadees fare well despite any combination of extreme cold or deep snow. For the most part their food is the larvae or the eggs that are deposited here and there in the tree by hundreds of kinds of insects and parasites which afflict trees. Nothing except a heavy sleet appears to make these food deposits inaccessible.

Most birds spend the winter months in the South. However, bad conditions may cause resident birds and animals to migrate, even in midwinter. Extremely unfavorable winters in British Columbia will cause many birds that regularly winter in that country to travel one or two thousand miles southward into the mountains of Colorado. Among the species which thus modify their habits are the red crossbill, the redpoll, the Lapland longspur, and the snowy owl.

After all, there are points in common between the animal life of the wild and the human life of civilization. Man and the wild animals alike find their chief occupation in getting food or in keeping out of danger. Change plays a large part in the life of each, and abnormal conditions affect them both. Let a great snow come in early winter, and both will have trouble, and both for a time may find the struggle for existence severe.

The primitive man slaughtered stormbound animals, but civilized man rescues them. A deep snow offers a good opportunity for more intimate acquaintance with our wild neighbors. And snowy times, too, are good picture taking periods. In snowy times, if our wild neighbors already respect us, tempting food and encouraging hunger will place big, shy, and awkward country fellows and nervous birds close to the camera and close to our hearts.

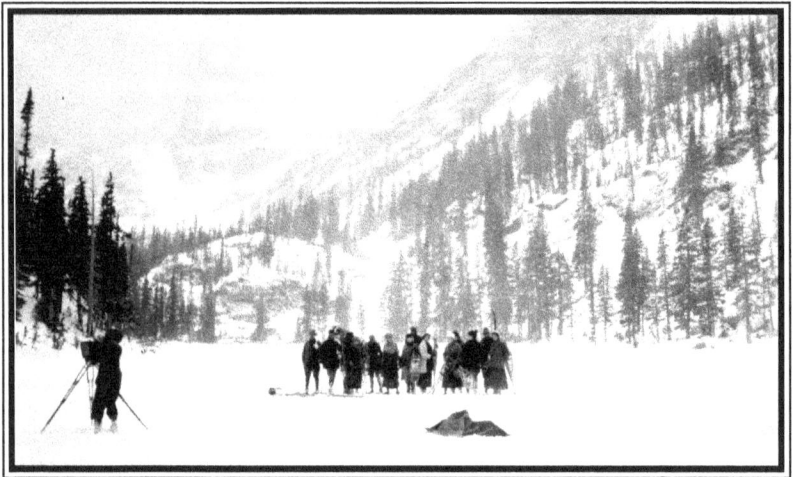

Esther Burnell Mills and a group enjoy a winter day at Fern Lake, Rocky Mountain National Park.

The woods are lovely, dark and deep, but I have promised to keep, and miles to go before I sleep.
    Robert Frost

Winter Mountaineering

After a heavy snowfall one December morning, I started on skis for two weeks' camping in the Colorado Rockies. The fluffy snow lay smooth and unbroken over the broken mountains. Here and there black pine and spruce trees uplifted arrowheads and snow cones of the white mantle. On the steep slope, half a mile from my cabin, I was knocked to one side by a barrel mass of snow dropping upon me from a tree, and one ski escaped. As if glad to be off on an adventure of its own, it sped down the mountainside like a shot. It bumped into a low stump, skied high into the air and over a treetop, and then fell undamaged in the deep snow.

Recovering my runaway ski, I started for the summit of the range, a distance of about nine miles from my cabin. For an hour I followed a stream whose swift waters now and then splashed up through the broken, icy skylights. Then leaving the canyon and skirting the slope, I was on the plateau summit of the Continental Divide, twelve thousand feet above the sea.

This summit moor was deeply overlaid with undrifted snow. Southward it extended mile after mile, rising higher and higher into the sky in broken, snow-covered peaks. To the north the few small broken cliffs and low buttes emphasized the trackless solitude. This plateau or moorland was less than one mile wide and comparatively smooth. Its edges descended precipitously two thousand feet into cirques and canyons.

Southward I traveled along the nearly level expanse of undrifted snow. Looking back along the line of my ski tracks, I saw a mountain lion leisurely cross from east to west. Apparently she had come up out of the woods for mad play and slaughter among the unfortunate snow-bound folk of the summit. She stopped at my tracks for an interested look, turned her head, and glanced back along the way I had come. Then her eyes appeared to follow my tracks to the boulder pile from behind which

I was then looking.

Playfully bouncing off the snow, she struck into my ski prints with one forepaw, lightly as a kitten. Then she dived into them, pretended to pick up something between her forepaws, reared, and with a swing tossed it into the air. Then her playful mood changed and she started on across the Divide. After several steps she stopped, looking back as if she had forgotten something but was a little too lazy to retrace her steps. But finally she came back. She walked along my ski tracks for a few steps, then began to romp, now and then making a great leap forward, and rolled and struck about with the pretense of worrying something she had captured. She repeated this pantomime a few times, and then, as if suddenly remembering her original plan of action, again walked westward. Arriving at the summit she hesitated, and when I saw her last she was calmly surveying the scenes far below.

On the mountain skyline I crossed a white tundra, half expecting to see an Eskimo peer from a snow mound. Arctic plants buried in the snow and ptarmigan— "Eskimo chickens"—in their snow-white dress were the only signs of life. Later in the day I saw a white weasel slipping over the snow toward a number of the ptarmigan. Often on the summits the ptarmigan, in leggings and coats of pure white, watched me and allowed me to come and remain near. They, like the snowshoe rabbit, skimmed over the surface on home-grown snowshoes. Possibly from them the Eskimos got the idea for the webbed snowshoe, which they have used for ages. More than once, when weathering gales were thick, insistent snow dust made me acquainted with the unpleasant sensations of strangulation, I have envied the rosy finch and other birds of the snow who have a well-developed screen to keep choking snow dust out of the nostrils. The Eskimos also have a slotted wooden shield to protect the eye from the burning glare of reflected sunlight.

I descended a few hundred feet into the upper edge of the woods to find shelter for the night. Clearing out the snow between a cliff and a rock about six feet from it, I had an excellent lodging place. I built a roaring fire and heated a number of stones. When this space was warmed I pushed the fire and the heated stones along the open space between the rock and the cliff. Then I started a fire against the base of the detached rock. Two huge sticks were placed at the bottom of this fire pile. Over these smaller

Enos' younger brother, Enoch "Joe" Mills, on a
boulder overlooking Long's Peak and Tahosa Valley.

ones were laid, and at the top still smaller ones. I set fire to this on the top so that it would burn slowly and not be at its hottest for an hour or two. Within the circle of warmth I placed my elkskin sleeping bag, crawled into it, and slept for nearly four hours. When the cold awakened me I renewed both fires, then had another short sleep. When I again awoke I was ready for another day's adventure.

I set off through a forested slope that tilted gently toward the sun. Black shadows, long and straight, lay upon the forest floor. The crowded pines were slender and limbless except at the top. Across an opening these slender shadows were at their best, with the snow glistening in white lines between their deep black ones. After two hours I came out upon a white and treeless meadow, across which shadows were flying—moving cloud shadows rushed across, and the shadow of a soaring eagle appeared swiftly skating in circles over the snow.

I spent hours reading the news, observing the illustrations, and studying the hieroglyphics on the snow. Whether footprints in the mud or snow may have suggested printing cannot be told, but it is certain that the tracks, stains and impressions in snow print the news and record the local animal doings. Here the rabbits played; there the grouse searched for dinner; while over yonder the long, lacy trail of a mouse ends significantly between the impressions of two wing feathers. One sees a trail made by a long-legged animal and another by a fellow with a long body and short legs—perhaps a weasel. At one place near the foot of an old tree a squirrel had abandoned a cone and run home. Nearby was the trail of a porcupine who was well-fed, well-protected, and though dull-witted, not at all afraid. Apparently he hadn't any idea where he was going and did not care whom he should meet; for at one place he came face to face with a fox and the fox turned aside.

Footprints often reveal the excitement, hesitation, change of plan, and the preparation of two wild folks advancing and about to meet. Most animals, except the grizzly, though concerned with sight and scent, appear not to consider the impressions in the tell-tale snow.

I passed again through woods where the previous winter I had walked upon ten feet of snow. In that trip I had looked down upon a camp-bird cuddled in an old nest. I talked to her for a minute, and, as is common with her kind, she came close, seeking something to eat. Three eggs were in the nest, though it was February. Never before had I found a bird nesting in the famine month of the year. These eggs may not have hatched, but another time I saw a nest of this species in March with eggs that did hatch. April is the nesting time for this bird. Why a pair sometimes nest unusually early is their secret.

I found the crested jay, that flings forth its jarring note as harsh and cold as frosty steel, using these mountains for winter quarters. A few of this species remain for the summer, but the majority nest farther north. The water ouzel is a winter songster, and twice during this outing, in a snow-filled canyon, he sang to me cheerily. He may be seen and heard in any month of the year. This bird of quiet, cheering presence is an outdoor enthusiast. He was always delightfully busy, and indifferent to my close approach if I came quietly and slowly.

The scarlet berries and small, shining green leaves of the kinnikinick gave color and charm to many snowy places. Half buried in the snow, in the sun or shadow, in niches of crags, or as wreath-like coverings for the rocks, they were bright and cheerful everywhere.

I can imagine that the winter birds and animals worship the chinook wind. One evening I went to sleep shivering. I was awakened through being too warm, and leaped out of my sleeping bag thinking it must be on fire. Then I discovered that in the night a chinook had come. This warm, dry wind occasionally follows a blizzard, and often it appears to make a sudden and triumphant attack upon a cold period. During the short day or two that it dominates it is a blessing. It often raises the temperature thirty or more degrees in a few hours.

On another cold, windy night I had a poor camp and damp clothes. I had examined the ice around a beaver house to see if it was built by a spring. It was, and I had broken through the thin ice. That night as I shivered by a slow fire I wished that I might have occupied a woodpecker's house. I took comfort in the fact that at no time during the trip would I be annoyed by flies or mosquitoes.

From the sheltering edge of the woods I watched the high wind stir and sweep the excited snow. The snowflakes had long since been reduced to powder and dust by colliding with cliffs and by being thrown violently against the earth. The wind was intermittent. A wave of snow dust swept along the snow-crusted earth, filling the air; then a few seconds of sunshine played before the next wave followed. Occasionally everything cleared and stopped for an exhibit of the whirlwind. A towering white column of snow dust would spin across the scene. This commonly was followed by another and heavier spiral that was more like a confusion of white whirled clouds. All this time the sun was shining in a blue sky; and all this time, too, a sparkling pennant of diamond snow dust and powder a mile long was fluttering from the tip of a triangular peak.

With such scenes in mind—the trees abloom with flakes, the white and sparkling whirlwinds, the vast and scintillating snow-powder pennants—I could understand the poetic fancy of primitive people who happily named the winter's gifts "snow-flowers" and who honored the snow period with an outdoor celebration.

After all, winter is but a transient return of the ice age. With fresh falls on the heights above timberline, before the wind blows, the vast world appears overlaid with a permanent stratum of snow. Across white distances one looks for miles without seeing a tree or any living object or even a shadow unless it be that of a passing cloud.

Though the high mountains have their snowstorms and their eternal snowfields, in most mountain ranges the snowfall on the middle slopes of the mountains is heavier than upon the high plateaus and summits. On the heights the wind has free play and sweeps most of the snow into enormous piles or drifts. These are one hundred or more feet deep and sometimes cover nearly a square mile. Owing to their depth, the low temperature of the heights, and the fact that they are so densely packed, these snow masses endure throughout the year. Wind is thus the chief factor in the making of snow topography. Small hills and plains, canyons, plateaus, and mountain ranges—all of snow—are a constant source of interest.

One morning I awoke with dense, white storm clouds all around me and the snow coming down. Wishing to camp that night at timberline, I traveled up the mountainside in the thickly falling snow and dense clouds. These clouds were drifting easily along the mountainside and, together with the feathery flakes which they were shedding, made it impossible to see distinctly even to the end of an extended arm. Suddenly I became aware of a diminished depth of snow underfoot. I stooped to measure it. It was less than three inches. On rising I thrust my head through the silver lining—the upper surface—of the cloud into the sunshine.

The altitude was about eleven thousand feet. Above and about me the peaks and plateaus stood in gray and brown. Not a flake of all this snow had fallen upon them. There was nothing to indicate that a storm had prevailed just below during the last two days and nights, or that only a step down the mountain snow was still falling.

Soundless and motionless the cloud sea lay below. Here and there an upthrusting pinnacle cast a shadow upon it. Unable to make myself believe that below me the flakes were falling thick and fast and that the ground was deeply covered with soft white snow, I plunged down into the cloud. After enjoying the novelty for a few minutes I climbed out of the snowstorm again and then once more descended into it. As the mountainside was comparatively unbroken I walked along the upper edge of the cloud for some distance. Two or three times this fluffy mass swelled and rose slightly above me and then settled easily back. In the head of a gulch cloud swells rose slightly higher than out in the main sea. I climbed down into them a short distance, thinking to cross the hidden canyon, but, finding it too steep-walled, climbed out again.

As I emerged from the gulch I saw, nearby, a huge grizzly bear sunning himself on a cliff that rose a few feet out of the cloud into the sunshine. He, like myself, appeared greatly interested in the slow rise and fall and ragged outline of the storm cloud. He was all attention to every new movement near him. On scenting me he stared for a moment, as if thinking: "Where on earth did he come from?" Then he stepped overboard into the clouds.

I camped that night beside a clump of storm-battered trees that marked the upper limit of the forest. In the morning all was clear. The cloud sea of the day before had rolled silently away. Along the mountainside the ragged edge of snow stretched for miles. Above it barren, rocky peaks rose in a great mountain desert. Below, all was soft and white—a wonderful world of mountains made of snowflakes.

Near my camp was an ancient looking tree clump. None of the trees was taller than my head, and though of almost normal form they were somewhat gnarled and appeared as old as the hills. Centuries they surely had seen. Trees on the forest outpost in high mountains endure severe trials. They are dwarfed, battered, and broken; huddled behind boulders, buried, or half buried in snow. The forest frontier is maintained by these brave tree people. Seen again and again, this region displays features of new interest as often as the visitor returns to it.

On the heights I frequently saw conies. One day I lingered to watch one that was less shy than the majority. He sat with his back against the sunny side of a boulder, looking serious and keeping a careful survey of his field of vision. Presently I discovered his haystack—his supply of winter food—a tiny heap of grass, sedge, and alpine plants. It was about two feet high and was sheltered beneath two half-arching stones.

Many were the ways in which I found animals spending the winter. In the course of this outing I saw several flocks of mountain sheep. All these were in the heights above the tree line. On the day following the snow-drifting one I crossed the heights and on the summit passed close to a flock. They were feeding in a space that the wind had swept bare of snow. Happy highlanders they were, well fed and contented, in their home twelve thousand feet above the tides.

One sunny, though cold, morning I came upon a large, dead tree. In it were a number of woodpecker holes. Wondering if these houses had winter dwellers I struck the tree with my hatchet. Instantly a dozen or more chickadees came pouring out of one of the holes like so many merry children. From a hole in the opposite side to the tree flew one or more birds that I did not see. Out of one of the upper holes a downy wood-pecker thrust his head. Glaring down at me with one eye—impatient, as late sleepers usually are when called—he appeared to be wanting to say: "Why am I disturbed? This is a cold morning. There are no early worms to be had in winter." From another hole flew another downy. I felt sure that none of these late sleepers had breakfasted. Seldom is an old woodpecker house without a tenant. Bluebirds, wrens, and numbers of weak-billed folk nest in them during summer, while birds of other species find them lifesavers in the winter. A hummingbird's nest that I found brought to mind the fact that its builder, if alive, was then among the tropical flowers of Central America.

Later in the day I saw a flock of chickadees, one or two brown creepers, and a solitary woodpecker food hunting together. The chickadees kept up a cheering conversation and twice I thought I heard the woodpecker give a call. I wondered if these fellow food hunters also all lodged in one many-roomed apartment house.

Coming one day to a beaver pond I scraped off the snow and looked through the clear ice into the water. Two or three beavers were swimming. The water between the ice and the bottom of the pond was about two feet deep. Each autumn the beavers pile ample winter supplies in deep water close to the house. The pond may freeze over, but this ice covering is a protection. The house entrance is on the bottom of the pond beneath the ice, and the floor is above the level of the pond. The water in the lower part of the house does not freeze. The beaver residents were here having a comfortable time while deer in nearby woods were floundering in the snow. I have known deer to have a hard time of it in winter. Commonly deer winter in lower altitudes, but sometimes they stay in the middle mountain region and worry through the snowy weeks by yarding—that is, a number remaining in one small area, where through daily trampling they keep on top of the snow and still find enough to eat.

A number of animals hibernate. Fat woodchucks live in a den five or six feet below the surface. Storms may come and go, but the woodchuck sleeps till the first flowers wake. The grizzly and black bear spend from three to five months in heavy, hibernating sleep.

Plants, too, though anchored, have a variety of winter customs. Trees may be said to hibernate, even the firs and spruces that go to sleep in full dress. Beneath the snow are countless seeds that will live their life next year, and numbers of plants that have hauled down their towers and colors for the winter. You may seek them and walk over them, and Mother Nature will only say: "Trouble me not, for the door is now shut and my children are with me in bed."

Moss in midwinter is as fresh and charming as though knee-deep in June. It is dainty and striking in a white setting. Mosses and lichens are ever a part of the poetry associated with ferns and the golden sands of bubbling springs; they are sharers in the cheerful, ever-silent beauty of the wild. They never intrude, but are among the most subdued and harmonious decorations in all nature. Yet lichens carry all the colors of the rainbow. In dark woods, deep canyons, and on the pinnacles of high peaks they cling in leafy, maplike decoration of oxidized silver, hammered brass, pure copper, and stains of yellow, brown, scarlet, gray, and green. They are almost classical decorations and touch with soft color and beauty the roughest bark and boulders. Until one knows that they are living things

The Street Family,
Colorado pioneers,
with their winter
equipment.

they seem only chemical colorings on the crags, and a part of the color scheme in the bark of trees.

One day during this outing I had been walking in the shadow of a mountain, which, together with the darkness of the spruce woods, made the snow almost a gray expanse. As I climbed out of the shadow on to a plateau, just at sunset, how splendidly, dazzlingly white was the skyline of peaks! On this white and broken line the sunset-colored clouds strangely rested. A sunset is never an old story, and a colored sunset above the white west line of winter's silent earth renews the imagination of youth.

Though I crossed a number of alpine lakes they were not to be seen. They were gone from the landscape. A stratum of marble instead of snow could not better have concealed them. Lakes, flowers, and bears were asleep for the winter.

In snowless places the brooks had decorated their ways with beautiful ice structures—arches and arcades, spires and frozen splashes, and endless stretches and forms of silver streamside platings and boulder drapings; ice, crystal clear, frosted and opaque. Many rocks were overspread with ice sheets and icy drapery, and cliffs were decked with fretwork and stupendous icicles. Smaller streams froze to the bottom, overflowed and out-built. In places wide areas were covered to enormous depths. Looking upon these one might almost fancy the Ice Age returning. But three months later the ice was gone to the far-off sea, and the flowers that slept beneath were massing their brilliant blossoms in the sun.

An old Ute chief once told me that during the hardest winter he had ever known in his country the snow for weeks lay "six ponies deep." The average annual snowfall in the Rocky Mountains is less than twenty-five feet. This is less than the average for the Alps.

Meetings with other human beings were few. One day, while walking down a plateau, I saw a dark figure that stood waiting on the edge of a snowy mountain moor a mile distant. As I approached the man waved an arm to attract my attention and when I came near enough he said by way of greeting:

"I thought you had not seen me."

We were above the limits of tree growth, and below and about us was a wild array of peaks and canyons.

"When I saw you come racing down that peak shoulder," said the man, "I fancied that you were an escaping Siberian convict, sentenced for political aims. What is your sentence or your service?"

"They call me the Snow Man," I replied. "I am making winter experiments and gathering information along the summit of the Continental Divide." I had not as yet become official "Colorado Snow Observer."

In answer to a counter question of mine he said:

"Oh, I'm a prospector, fifty-four, born in Ireland, raised in Australia and Siberia. Am after gold in Spruce Gulch. If I don't strike it by spring I'm off for Alaska. Stirring reports from there."

It was a good place to look around. Several towering peaks were strangely near. A number of summits reached up fourteen thousand feet into the blue sky. Colorado is crowded with a vast and wondrous array of mountains. Many of these are united by narrow plateaus that are savagely side-cut with deep canyons. Each time I gained a commanding height I looked again and again, awed by the immensity of it all, at peaks and canyons with their broken strata of snow.

This outing, as usual, was all too short. Ten of its fourteen days were sunny and calm. Through two days the wind roared. Two other days were filled with snowstorms. Each day I went to some new scene. I climbed one fourteen-thousand-foot peak. I occupied one camp three nights, but on each of the other nights I had a new camp. Most of the nights were filled with stars, and always there was the blazing campfire. On my way home I met a man who had heard of my winter camping habits. After questioning me concerning the objects of interest seen, he asked:

"Is this a good time of year for a vacation?"

I replied:

"A good time for a vacation is whenever you can spare the time, and the very best time for a vacation in the mountains is when you can stay the longest."

Nature never hurries: atom by atom, little by little, she achieves her work.

Ralph Waldo Emerson

R u n n i n g   D o w n   G l a c i e r s

For many years, the mountain people of Switzerland asked the question, "Do glaciers move?" Then a glacier without warning came down out of its canyon across a meadow and pushed a barn over. That glacier had its proper standing. A little later, another glacier moved down and chased the workmen out of a marble quarry. Elsewhere in the Alps, about the same time, a man built a small hut upon a glacier. In due time this hut was moved forward by the ice and traveled with the glacier more than a mile. These incidents, together with the measurements of scientists, settled the question. Glaciers move.

The entire southern coast of Alaska has been shaped by glaciers, and when I visited Alaska in the summer of 1892, any number were still sliding from the steep, snowy mountains into the sea. These young bergs, many of them of enormous size, rolled ponderously about, bowing profoundly and making a stir as they entered the world-round sea.

I was looking for glaciers, and here seemed to be a splendid world's fair exhibit on them. While watching one from close range, it shed off a huge berg. This bobbed up and rolled heavily over. The high wave that it sent far up the shore threw driftwood about like a flood, and carrying me along with it, finally pitched me headlong at the line of high tide.

Coming upon a big berg becalmed in a small harbor with its snout inclined against the shore, I concluded to climb up. It rose fifty or sixty feet above water, and had a plateau surface. A few steps had to be chopped, but with little difficulty I reached the top. It was nearly level and about four hundred feet long, though less than one hundred wide. In one spot were several well-rounded boulders like big eggs in a nest. These were ready to roll overboard. A flat triangular-shaped stone was supported several feet above the common level by a triangular ice mass which the stone had shaded and thus delayed its melting. A number of boulders like large peanuts were set in the ice. A few carloads of sand and gravel were frozen on and in the offshore end. Apparently a gravel-laden stream, while the berg still had a place in a glacier, had poured down upon it. There were no deep cracks, and if there had been ancient crevasses, these had been closed and mended to as to defy detection.

What most interested me was a pile of confused logs partly embedded in the top and one side of the berg. These were mostly of broken spruce trees and probably had been swept down upon the glacier by a snow slide. I had carried my bear skin and another blanket up with me, so I concluded to have a night at the top. The logs burned well, and my rousing fire lighted the spruce-walled shore. Knowing that a heavy swell or something else might start the berg on an adventure out to sea, I was careful to watch for any unusual movement, and ever listened for sounds of rising or surging waters. Perhaps the chief reason for spending a night on this iceberg was Youth.

Just how many billion snowflakes were compressed in this ice cake could not be figured. If it had been assembled and started from the extreme wing of the canyon down which it had apparently slid, and had slid forward 1,000 feet per year, the journey to tide water had required eighty-four years. Its descent from source to sea was about nine hundred feet.

Many a glacier never reaches the sea, and may be likened to a desert stream that evaporates and disappears in the sand. In a wet year, such a stream flows beyond the ordinary place of disappearance, while in a dry year it does not reach this place.

With a big fire burning, I lay down for a sleep. I had figured that I could get off the berg quickly in case it suddenly started out to sea. Of course, I might have to swim, but the shore was close. Strangely, with marvelous distinctness shone the stars, and I was alone, a stranger in a Past of several thousand years ago.

Though chilled, I awoke with the fires of sunrise blazing into the sky behind the black mountain wall. The berg's restlessness had awakened me. When I was less than a quarter of a mile along the shore, the berg did put out to sea.

There are only a few small glaciers in the Rockies, but small as they are, a visit to their blue-green ice piles in midsummer stirs the imagination. The number of glacier meadows and the numerous well-preserved old moraines easily enable one to form a picture of the region during the Ice Age. Most of the canyons in the Continental Divide which lie in altitudes of from eight to thirteen thousand feet have glacier-polished walls.

At one place in the Rocky Mountains, I saw a small glacier at an altitude of 13,000 feet, which was evidently in a wind eddy near the summit of the range. Apparently, it was maintained entirely by the snow which the wind blew to it. This snow had come from off an area above the timberline which aggregated about four square miles. In this and other instances, a change of direction in the prevailing wind, and the glacier would vanish.

In the Rocky Mountain National Park, the few remaining glaciers are on the east side of the Continental Divide. On the west side of the Divide there is a heavier snowfall, but there are no glaciers. The cause of this condition is prevailing westerly winds. These sweep much of the snow from the upper western slopes and the summit and deposit it in the upper ends of the canyons with the "eternal snowfields" on the eastern side.

Commonly, a glacier is formed in the upper end of a canyon by the vast quantity of snow which slides down off tributary slopes and is swept to it by the wind—even the snow which blows off the other side of the mountain.

Wherever more snow falls or accumulates each year than melts, an icy mass will result, and in due time there will be a movement of this ice. The steepness of the slope will determine the quantity which is required to produce a movement. On a steep slope, a moderate quantity will move. Weight and rapid melting compact snowdrifts into ice. Ice under pressure becomes plastic, and where a few hundred feet are up-piled, the weight of the top is too great for the bottom layers to withstand, and it is squeezed out.

The main motive power of a glacier is the downgrade pull of gravity. The expansion and push due to freezing also advance it. The pressure of the up-piled weight at the source is also felt all along the line.

Glaciers—ice piles—move for the same reason that causes snow piles to slip and slide, because they were dropped or formed on a slope so steep that they were ever slipping.

On the upper end of a glacier in Glacier Bay, I found a mountainous

Two men climb a steep snowfield above timberline.
Photograph by Dean Babcock.

mass of snow, near-ice, piled upon the glacier. This accumulation of several snow slides, one or more of which appeared to have come down each of the several gulches, all united on the glacier. This was the source and resource of the glacier.

This mighty pile rested upon a foundation of glacier ice which filled the canyon below. This foundation could not support its weight of snow and ice, and constantly slipped and slid forward down the canyon. Storms, winds, and snow slides maintain the glacier reservoir, supply the pressure, and thus sustain the flow—the downward, forward movement of the glacier.

In a number of places, glaciers have traveled part of their way up grade, up a slope and over a ridge. The inconceivable pressure of the enormous and elevated masses of ice at their upper reaches and sources had forced the flow forward.

In the Yosemite National Park, the ancient Tenaya Glacier flowed westerly from the summits of the Sierras. It left a strange and impressive story of the ways and the work of ice. It was about two miles wide, more than fourteen miles long, and in places two thousand feet deep. Between Tuolumne and Tenaya basins, it slid up a steep slope, climbing five hundred feet, received a tributary, then poured over against Clouds Rest and down upon the domes of the Yosemite.

What a wild, grand sight this rough, wide, deep ice stream must have made as it swept onward and downward from the summit of the Sierras! Mount Hoffman, miles in front of the range, split this grand ice stream as a rocky island splits a river. One fork of this ice veered off to descend and work out the sculpturing in Hetch-Hetchy. The other gave its attention to the Yosemite, climbed up a steep, was joined by a tributary stream, where it went over the top, and then descended to help shape the stupendous and splendid rock sculpture through the length of the Yosemite Valley.

The weight of a glacier, especially along its upper, deeper reaches, is enormous. Usually, the upper part is laden with large quantities of rock and landslide material. The vast up-piled ice and stones cause the glacier to bear heavily on the bottom of the canyon and to exert against its walls a telling pressure, sometimes aggregating one hundred tons per square foot.

This rough mass of ice and stones, moving under enormous pressure, enables it to cut all touched surfaces away. Its erosive force is enormous. The mass of ice mingled with rocks moves slowly forward, tearing off projecting rocks from the walls and from the bottom of the canyon; it rasps, planes, and polishes all surfaces touched. When a glacier continues to flow for thousands of years, as glaciers have frequently done, it greatly deepens and widens its channel, smooths and wears off the surface over which it travels. Rough V-shaped canyons are smoothed, deepened, and made U-shaped. Mountain peaks are planed down to low turtle outlines, and low-lying hills are leveled off into plains.

The glacier's erosive power appears greatest headward. A glacier sometimes temporarily freezes fast at the source; a lurch and forward movement, and the frozen upper end drags out rocks of many tons. It thus works its way headward into and often through a mountain. Had the Ice Age lasted another century, Longs Peak might have lost the remaining part of its head.

The nose or front of a glacier made up of ice, and ofttimes an equal quantity of stones, has a formidable appearance. It is effective in ploughing and cutting its way. Where a glacier descends a steep slope and comes in contact with a level stretch, it commonly bears down and cuts deeply, thus forming a basin of solid rock, which, after the melting away of the ice, is filled with water. Most mountain lakes occupy basins that were formed in this manner. The Rocky Mountains, the Cascades, and the Sierras owe their numerous lakes to glacial action. The most beautiful lakes in New York State, in the Glacier National Park, those in Scotland, and, in fact, the overwhelming majority of the lakes of the world, repose in rock basins which were scooped out by the slow, vigorous action of glacial ice, or they rest in reservoirs that were formed by glacial moraines damming a section of a former river channel or a previously cut canyon. Hudson Bay was probably excavated by glaciers.

Wisconsin is dotted with lakes of glacial origin, and many of its lakes repose in depressions of glacial drift. The Great Lakes are glacial. A number of the long, narrow lakes of New York State are parts of old river channels. Of course, a few of the lakes of the world were formed in basins produced by landslide debris, clogged river channels, or in the former fiery and abandoned craters of volcanoes.

Exploring a crevasse in Rowe Glacier.

In the Rocky Mountains there are innumerable meadows and valleys in which flourish forest, grasses, and flowers in the soil ground for plant food by the glaciers. This soil comes chiefly from the ground-up rock—the rock flour—which results from the grind of glacial movement. Possibly one half the soil now serving over the earth is traceable to glacial origin. Soil was in part distributed by glaciers and further outspread by the action of wind and water. Many of the more extensive and productive grain-growing areas in the United States have glacial soil. Many farms districts in Canada and Europe are in glacial drift. And thus we may say that one of the prime resources of the earth—soil—which now makes the earth livable, is the great rock grist which the glaciers ground and transported and which wind and water and the chemistry of nature made ready and widely distributed.

But in addition to these activities, glaciers have given flowing lines to landscapes, have beautified the earth with rounded hills, and have decorated it with lakes of exquisite beauty and water basins of every form and size. A majority of the Sierra landscapes are new, recently made by glaciers, and nearly all the forests in the Sierras and the Rocky Mountains are growing on glacial moraines.

John Muir long ago pointed out that the gentle, delicate snowflake—a snow flower—is a rock trimming and polishing agency of importance, an earth artist of first magnitude. When one thinks of glaciers he must necessarily think of landscapes, soil, and scenery.

In a moving glacier, its front and bottom and sides are set with innumerable cutting tools in the form of broken rocks. These rocks wear out or become dulled, and as they advance in the ice of the glacier, are dropped in the lateral moraines or dumped at the terminals. The ice has continuous flow and the landslides from the heights are frequently dropping whole trainloads of new tools—broken rock—upon the glacier. Then, too, the glacier is constantly seizing rocky material at the head or tearing it from the sides and bottom of the canyon. Running water, too, covers and fills ice full of sand and gravel. This also helps to cut and polish the floor and walls of the canyon.

After a glacier has flowed through the same channel for a thousand or more years, it has measurably straightened, widened, and deepened this channel. The ice may then melt away, but its enormous carving remains, and in the lateral and terminal moraines and in the outspread silt drift and soil may be had a glimpse of the material which it moved.

On one glacier, vegetation was growing in the soil of a rock garden. This showed a number of flowers in bloom, alpine gentians, yellow avens, and purple primroses. On the edge of a crevasse nearby rested a number of arctic ptarmigan. A cony was squeaking among the rocks, while on the nearby ice a number of rosy finches were feeding.

In places, I have found wild animals well preserved though long dead in the terminus of a glacier. They evidently had fallen into crevasses possibly a hundred or more years before, and has lain in cold storage through all the years. Most material that falls into crevasses is likely to be crushed or to be ground up as the ice advances over its uneven bed.

A glacier, like a river, transports vast quantities of material, mostly rocky debris. This usually starts in the form of rocks, which are ground to flour, pebbles, cobblestones, and boulders. The material eroded and carried forward by the glacier may fill in canyons over which it is passing or finally be dumped at the terminus of the glacier. At the lower end or terminus of a glacier, where all the ice melts away, quantities of this rock debris is dropped, and is called a terminal moraine. In many a glacier, this would amount to hundreds of tons daily.

Terminal moraines of vast size may be seen in the mountains and also in the Mississippi Valley. Much of the area of Iowa, Dakota, Minnesota, Wisconsin, Illinois, Indiana, and Ohio is overlaid with glacial drift and morainal matter from ten feet to five hundred feet deep.

The topography of the greater part of the Northern Hemisphere has been carved chiefly by glaciers. Canada has undergone vast and inconceivable changes from ice erosion, and the northern surface of the United States was wrought mainly by glacial forces. They have cut thousands of mountain canyons, enlarged and reshaped others, dressed mountain ranges down to plains.

By dumping or depositing vast quantities of morainal debris, glaciers sometimes fill a valley and extinguish a stream or change the direction of the water flow.

The Missouri River formerly flowed northeast and perhaps emptied somewhere to the northwest of Lake Superior. This lake went out of existence, and the Missouri River was broadly pushed a few hundred miles to the south, and its waters made connection with the Mississippi River.

Long Island is a terminal moraine, the delta of an ice river that was piled during the last Ice Age. The material was scraped and transported from the mountains of New York, New England, and Canada. This stupendous mass of material will give some idea of the inconceivable quantity of debris which glaciers accumulate, transport, and distribute.

A glacier may terminate—melt away—at about the same place year after year and pile up an enormous terminal moraine. A few years of scanty snows, and it will retreat; that is, its lower end will melt away without reaching the old terminal place. If there comes more than ordinary snowfall, the glacier will in due time respond, and its end plough through the deposited moraine delta and push beyond the ordinary terminal point.

If a glacier moves five or six feet per day—about two thousand feet per year—terminating each year at the same place, two thousand feet of it will melt away each year, and the weight or quantity of rock debris deposited each year will be the amount in the terminal two thousand feet.

After the glacier emerges from the canyon, the rock material in the sides of a glacier and on its top often rolls off and forms great embankments or levee-like ridges—lateral moraines, on each side of the ice stream. The Rocky Mountains and the Sierras carry thousands of these bouldery moraines, which in places look like extensions of canyon walls.

A boulder may have had strange, violent experiences. The original rock fragment may have been torn from a cliff which projected into the canyon, from the bottom or wall of the canyon, or have been plucked from the uppermost end of the canyon. It may have fallen from a skyline cliff and tumbled down upon the glacier where, for a time, it was carried on the surface. Later, it may have dropped into a crevasse and reached the bottom. Here, wedged in the ice, its sharp corners and edges may have been brought in contact with the rock over which the glacier was sliding, and it may have gouged and rubbed against this under a pressure of one hundred or more tons per square foot. It was crushed, ground, rolled, scoured, and carved. By coming in contact with other rocks receiving similar treatment, it may have been pushed to the surface at the top or the side, to roll out upon the lateral moraine, or to become one of many in the terminal moraine.

The more spectacular America and European glaciers are long, narrow tongues of ice, commonly in a canyon. They may be one hundred feet or a mile wide, a mile or several miles long, and from a few feet to many hundred feet thick. Many of the existing glaciers are long, narrow ice rivers occupying gorges in the mountains.

The greatest glaciers on the continent are in Alaska. Greenland still is largely covered with an enormous glacier, and in the Antarctic, glaciers cover thousands of square miles to vast depth. The largest glacier in Switzerland is about ten miles long. There are glaciers in New Zealand, in the mountains of Asia, in the Andes, and one in Africa almost beneath the equator. Mount Rainier has splendid glaciers on its slope, the aggregate area of which is about fifty square miles. There are scores of glaciers in the mountains of Canada, numbers of small glaciers in the mountains of Canada, numbers of small glaciers in the Sierras of California, in the Rocky Mountain National Park, and in Glacier National Park.

All over the earth, for many years, because of lessened snowfalls, most glaciers have been retreating; that is to say, melting back at the lower end a little faster than they move forward. Here and there are exceptional conditions, perhaps increased snowfalls at its source, which cause a glacier to lengthen or advance.

The rate of movement in glaciers varies from a few feet per month to several feet per day. Generally the larger the glacier and the steeper its inclined channel, the faster it moves. In rare instances one may move forward twenty-five or thirty feet in a day.

Some tourists were one day looking at the terminus of a glacier and the guide was explaining that the glacier was moving forward a few feet each day—and also that the terminus had been at the same place for several years. "Evidently, then," said one of the tourists, "it is always moving, but never gets anywhere." A glacier travels gracefully. It is ever grinding soil and making landscapes.

There appear to have been at least five great Ice Ages during the long history of the earth. These have been levelers and have produced inconceivable topographical changes. The Great Ice Age, the most recent of the five, markedly changed all the northern part of North America.

It was in 1840 that Agassiz brought forward the Ice Age theory—

showed the recent glaciation of norther Europe and America. For nearly a generation, this now apparently obvious theory met with opposition. It is now almost universally believed by scientists.

One geologist has estimated that a permanent lowering of the temperature of five or possibly ten degrees in the temperate or arctic zones might bring on another Ice Age; and, too, a slightly increased snowfall in the north temperate zone might multiply the number of glaciers and increase the activity on the existing ones.

A crevasse in Rowe Glacier, Rocky Mountain National Park.

The ruddy clouds float in the four quarters of the cerulean sky.
And the white snowflakes show forth their six-petaled flowers.
  Hsiao Tung

Colorado Snow Observer

"Where are you going?" was the question asked me one snowy winter day. After hearing that I was off on a camping trip, to be gone several days, and that the place where I intended to camp was in deep snow on the upper slopes of the Rockies, the questioners laughed heartily. Knowing me, some questioners realized that I was in earnest, and all that they could say in the nature of argument or appeal was said to cause me to "forego the folly." But I went, and in the romance of a new world—on the Rockies in winter—I lived intensely through ten strong days and nights, and gave to my life new and rare experiences. Afterwards I made other winter excursions, all of which were stirring and satisfactory. The recollection of these winter experiences is as complete and exhilarating as any in the vista of my memory.

Some years after my first winter camping trip, I found myself holding a strange position—that of the "State Snow Observer of Colorado." I have never heard of another position like it. Professor L.G. Carpenter, the celebrated irrigation engineer, was making some original investigations concerning forests and the water supply. He persuaded me to take the position, and under his direction I worked as a government experiment officer. For three successive winters I traversed the upper slopes of the Rockies and explored the crest of the continent, alone. While on this work, I was instructed to make notes on "those things that are likely to be of interest or value to the Department of Agriculture or the Weather Bureau"—and to be careful not to lose my life.

On these winter trips I carried with me a camera, thermometer, barometer, compass, notebook, and folding axe. The food carried usually was only raisins. I left all bedding behind. Notwithstanding I was alone and in the wilds, I did not carry any kind of gun.

The work made it necessary for me to ramble the wintry heights in sunshine and storm. Often I was out, or rather up, in a blizzard, and on

Enos on a winter excursion.

more than one occasion I was out for two weeks on the snowdrifted crest of the continent, without seeing any one. I went beyond the trails and visited the silent places alone. I invaded gulches, eagerly walked the splendid forest aisles, wandered in the dazzling glare on dreary alpine moorlands, and scaled the peaks over mantles of ice and snow. I had many experiences—amusing, dangerous, and exciting. There was abundance of life and fun in the work. On many an evening darkness captured me and compelled me to spend the night in the wilds without bedding, and often without food. During these nights I kept a campfire blazing until daylight released me. When the night was mild, I managed to sleep a little—in installments—rising from time to time to give wood to the eager fire. Sometimes a scarcity of wood kept me busy gathering it all night; and sometimes the night was so cold that I did not risk going to sleep. During these nights I watched my flaming fountain of fire brighten, fade, surge, and change, or shower its spray of sparks upon the surrounding snow-flowers. Strange reveries I have had by these winter campfires. On a few occasions mountain lions interrupted my thoughts with their piercing, lonely cries; and more than once a reverie was pleasantly changed by the whisper of a chickadee in some nearby tree as a cold comrade snuggled up to it. Even during the worst of nights, when I thought of my lot at all, I considered it better than that of those who were sick in houses or asleep in the stuffy, deadly air of the slums.

> "Believe me, 't is something to be cast
> Face to face with thine own self at last."

Not all nights were spent outdoors. Many a royal evening was passed in the cabin of a miner or a prospector, or by the fireside of a family who for some reason had left the old home behind and sought seclusion in wild scenes, miles from neighbors. Among Colorado's mountains there are an unusual number of strong characters who are trying again. They are strong because broken plans, lost fortunes, or shattered health elsewhere have not ended their efforts or changed their ideals. Many are trying to restore health, some are trying again to prosper, others are just making a start in life, but there are a few who, far from the madding crowd, are living happily the simple life.

Sincerity, hope, and repose enrich the lives of those who live among the crags and pines of mountain fastness. Many a happy evening I have had with a family, or an old prospector, who gave me interesting scraps of autobiography along with a lodging for the night.

The snowfall on the mountains of Colorado is very unevenly distributed, and is scattered through seven months of the year. Two places only a few miles apart, and separated by a mountain range, may have very different climates, and one of these may have twice as much snowfall as the other. On the middle of the upper slopes of the mountains the snow sometimes falls during seven months of the year. At an altitude of eleven thousand feet the annual fall amounts to eighteen feet. This is several times the amount that falls at an altitude of six thousand feet. In a locality near Crested Butte the annual fall is thirty feet, and during snowy winters even fifty feet. Most winter days are clear, and the climate less severe than is usually imagined.

One winter I walked on snowshoes on the upper slopes of the "snowy" range of the Rockies, from the Wyoming line on the north to near the New Mexico line on the south. This was a long walk, and it was full of amusement and adventure. I walked most of the way on the crest of the continent. The broken nature of the surface gave me ups and downs. Sometimes I would descend to the level of seven thousand feet, and occasionally I climbed some peak that was fourteen thousand feet above the tides.

I had not been out many days on this trip when I was caught in a storm on the heights above treeline. I at once started downward for the woods. The way among the crags and precipices was slippery; the wind threatened every moment to hurl me over a cliff; the windblown snow filled the air so that I could see only a few feet, and at times not at all. But it was too cold to stop. For two hours I fought my way downward through the storm, and so dark it was during the last half hour that I literally felt my way with my staff. Once in the woods, I took off a snowshoe, dug a large hole in the snow down to the earth, built a fire, and soon forgot the perilous descent. After eating from my supply of raisins, I dozed a little, and woke to find all calm and the moon shining in glory on a snowy mountain world of peaks and pines. I put on my snowshoes, climbed upward beneath the moon, and from the summit of Lead

Mountain, thirteen thousand feet high, saw the sun rise in splendor on a world of white.

The tracks and records in the snow which I read in passing made something of a daily newspaper for me. They told much of news of the wilds. Sometimes I read of the games that the snowshoe rabbit had played; of a starving time among the brave mountain sheep on the heights; of the quiet content in the ptarmigan neighborhood; of the dinner that the pines had given the grouse; of the amusements and exercises on the deer's stamping ground; of the cunning of foxes; of the visits of magpies, the excursions of lynxes, and the red records of mountain lions.

The mountain lion is something of a game hog and an epicure. He prefers warm blood for every meal, and is very wasteful. I have much evidence against him; his worst one day record that I have shows five tragedies. In this time he killed a mountain sheep, a fawn, a grouse, a rabbit, and a porcupine; and as if this were not enough, he was about to kill another sheep when a dark object on snowshoes shot down the slope nearby and disturbed him. The instances where he has attacked human beings are rare, but he will watch and follow one for hours with the utmost caution and curiosity. One morning after a night journey through the wood, I turned back and doubled my trail. After going a short distance I came to the track of a lion alongside my own. I went back several miles and read the lion's movements. He had watched me closely. At every place where I rested he had crept up close, and at the place where I had sat down against a stump he had crept up to the opposite side of the stump—and I fear while I dozed!

One night during this expedition I had lodging in an old and isolated prospector's cabin, with two young men who had very long hair. For months they had been in seclusion, "gathering wonderful herbs," hunting out prescriptions for every human ill, and waiting for their hair to grow long. I hope they prepared some helpful, or at least harmless prescriptions, for, ere this, they have become picturesque, and I fear prosperous, medicine men on some populous street corner. One day I had dinner on the summit of Mt. Lincoln, fourteen thousand feet above the ocean. I ate with some miners who were digging out their fortune; and was "the only caller in five months."

But I was not always a welcome guest. At one of the big mining camps I stopped for mail and to rest for a day or so. I was all "rags and tags," and had several broken strata of geology and charcoal on my face in addition. Before I had got well into the town, from all quarters came dogs, each of which seemed determined to make it necessary for me to buy some clothes. As I had already determined to do this, I kept the dogs at bay for a time, and then sought refuge in a first class hotel; from this the porter, stimulated by an excited order from the clerk, promptly and literally kicked me out!

In the robings of winter how different the mountains than when dressed in the bloom of summer! In no place did the change seem more marked than on some terrace over which summer flung the lacy drapery of a white cascade, or where a wild waterfall "leapt in glory." These places in winter were glorified with the fine arts of ice—"frozen music" as someone has defined architecture—for here winter had constructed from water a wondrous array of columns, panels, filigree, fretwork, relief work, arches, giant icicles, and stalagmites as large as, and in many ways resembling, a big tree with a fluted full length mantle of ice.

Along the way were extensive areas covered with the ruins of fire-killed trees. Most of the forest fires which had caused these were the result of carelessness. The timber destroyed by these fires had been needed by thousands of home builders. The robes of beauty which they had burned from the mountain sides are a serious loss. These fire ruins preyed upon me, and I resolved to do something to save the remaining forests. The opportunity came shortly after the resolution was made.

Two days before reaching the objective point, farthest south, my food gave out, and I fasted. But as soon as I reached the end, I started to descend the heights, and very naturally knocked at the door of the first house I came to, and asked for something to eat. I supposed I was at a pioneer's cabin. A handsome, neatly dressed young lady came to the door, and when her eyes fell upon me she blushed and then turned pale. I was sorry that my appearance had alarmed her, but I repeated my request for something to eat. Just then, through the half-open door behind the young lady, came the laughter of children, and a glance into the room told me that I was before a mountain schoolhouse. By this time the teacher, to whom I was talking, startled me by inviting me in. As I sat eating a luncheon to which the teacher and each one of the six schoolchildren contributed, the teacher explained to me that she was recently from the East, and that I so well fitted her ideas of a Western desperado that she was frightened at first. When I finished eating, I made my first after-dinner speech; it was also my first attempt to make a forestry address. One point I tried to bring out was concerning the destruction wrought by forest fires. Among other things I said: "During the past few years in Colorado, forest fires which ought never to have started have destroyed many million dollars' worth of timber, and the area over which the fires have burned aggregates twenty-five thousand square miles. This area of forest would put on the equator an evergreen forest belt one mile wide that would reach entirely around the world. Along with this forest have perished many of the animals and thousands of beautiful birds who had homes in it."

I finally bade all goodbye, went on my way rejoicing, and in due course arrived at Denver, where a record of one of my longest winter excursions was written.

In order to give an idea of one of my briefer winter walks, I close this chapter with an account of a round trip snowshoe journey from Estes Park to Grand Lake, the most thrilling and adventurous that has ever entertained me on the trail.

One February morning I set off alone on snowshoes to cross the "range", for the purpose of making some snow measurements. The nature of my work for the State required the closest observation of the character and extent of the snow in the mountains. I hoped to get to Grand Lake for the night, but I was on the east side of the range, and Grand Lake was on the west. Along the twenty-five miles of trail there was only wilderness, without a single house. The trail was steep and the snow very soft. Five hours were spent in gaining timberline, which was only six miles from my starting place, but four thousand feet above it. Rising in bold grandeur above me was the summit of Long's Peak, and this, with the great hills of drifted snow, out of which here and there a dwarfed and distorted tree thrust its top, made timberline seem weird and lonely.

From this point the trail wound for six miles across bleak heights before it came down to timber on the other side of the range. I set forward as rapidly as possible, for the northern sky looked stormy. I must not only climb up fifteen hundred feet, but must also skirt the icy edges

Crest of the Continent.
12,200 feet above tide

"Cairn marking the contact
of the Atlantic and the Pacific
Slopes

Enos A. Mills
Estes Park, Colo

96

of several precipices in order to gain the summit. My friends had warned me that the trip was a foolhardy one even on a clear, calm day, but I was fated to receive the fury of a snowstorm while on the most broken portion of the trail.

The tempest came on with deadly cold and almost blinding violence. The wind came with awful surges, and roared and boomed among the crags. The clouds dashed and seethed along the surface, shutting out all landmarks. I was every moment in fear of slipping or being blown over a precipice, but there was no shelter; I was on the roof of the continent, twelve thousand five hundred feet above sea level, and to stop in the bitter cold meant death.

It was still three miles to timber on the west slope, and I found it impossible to keep the trail. Fearing to perish if I tried to follow even the general course of the trail, I abandoned it altogether, and started for the head of a gorge, down which I thought it would be possible to climb to the nearest timber. Nothing definite could be seen. The clouds on the snowy surface and the light electrified air gave the eye only optical illusions. The outline of every object was topsy-turvy and dim. The large stones that I thought to step on were not there; and, when apparently passing others, I bumped into them. Several times I fell headlong by stepping out for a drift and finding a depression.

In the midst of these illusions I walked out on a snow cornice that overhung a precipice! Unable to see clearly, I had no realization of my danger until I felt the snow giving way beneath me. I had seen the precipice in summer, and knew it was more than a thousand feet to the bottom! Down I tumbled, carrying a large fragment of the snow cornice with me. I could see nothing, and I was entirely helpless. Then, just as the full comprehension of the awful thing that was happening swept over me, the snow falling beneath me suddenly stopped. I plunged into it, completely burying myself. Then I, too, no longer moved downward; my mind gradually admitted the knowledge that my body, together with a considerable mass of the snow, had fallen upon a narrow ledge and caught there. More of the snow came tumbling after me, and it was a matter of some minutes before I succeeded in extricating myself.

When I thrust my head out of the snow mass and looked about me,

I was first appalled by a glance outward, which revealed the terrible height of the precipice on the face of which I was hanging. Then I was relieved by a glance upward, which showed me that I was only some twenty feet from the top, and that a return thither would not be very difficult. If I had walked from the top a few feet farther back, I should have fallen a quarter of a mile.

One of my snowshoes came off as I struggled out, so I took off the other shoe and used it as a scoop to uncover the lost web. But it proved very slow and dangerous work. With both shoes off I sank chest-deep in the snow; if I ventured too near the edge of the ledge, the snow would probably slip off and carry me to the bottom of the precipice. It was only after two hours of effort that the shoe was recovered.

When I first struggled to the surface of the snow on the ledge, I looked at once to find a way back to the top of the precipice. I quickly saw that by following the ledge a few yards beneath the unbroken snow cornice I could climb to the top over some jagged rocks. As soon as I had recovered the shoe, I started round the ledge. When I had almost reached the jagged rocks, the snow cornice caved upon me, and not only buried me, but came perilously near knocking me into the depths beneath. But at last I stood upon the top in safety.

A short walk from the top brought me out upon a high hill of snow that sloped steeply down into the woods. The snow was soft, and I sat down in it and slid "a blue streak"—my blue overalls recording the streak—for a quarter of a mile, and then came to a sudden and confusing stop; one of my webs had caught on a spine of one of the dwarfed and almost buried trees at timberline.

When I had traveled a short distance below timberline, a fearful crashing caused me to turn; I was in time to see fragments of snow flying in all directions, and snow-dust boiling up in a great geyser column. A snow-slide had swept down and struck a granite cliff. As I stood there, another slide started on the heights above timber, and with a far off roar swept down in awful magnificence, with a comet-like tail of snow-dust. Just at timberline it struck a ledge and glanced to one side, and at the same time shot up into the air so high that for an instant I saw the treetops beneath it. But it came back to earth with awful force, and I felt the ground tremble as it crushed a wide way through the woods. It finally brought up at the bottom of a gulch with a wreckage of hundreds of noble spruce trees that it had crushed down and swept before it.

As I had left the trail on the heights, I was now far from it and in a rugged and wholly unfrequented section, so that coming upon the fresh tracks of a mountain lion did not surprise me. But I was not prepared for what occurred soon afterward. Noticing a steamy vapor rising from a hole in the snow by the protruding roots of an overturned tree, I walked to the hole to learn the cause of it. One whiff of the vapor stiffened my hair and limbered my legs. I shot down a steep slope, dodging trees and rocks. The vapor was rank with the odor from a bear.

At the bottom of the slope I found the frozen surface of a stream much easier walking than the soft snow. All went well until I came to some rapids, where, with no warning whatever, the thin ice dropped me into the cold current among the boulders. I scrambled to my feet, with the ice flying like broken glass. The water came only a little above my knees, but as I had gone under the surface, and was completely drenched, I made an enthusiastic move toward the bank. Now snowshoes are not adapted for walking either in swift water or among boulders. I realized this thoroughly after they had several times tripped me, sprawling, into the liquid cold. Finally I sat down in the water, took them off, and came out gracefully.

I gained the bank with chattering teeth and an icy armor. My pocket thermometer showed two degrees above zero. Another storm was bearing down upon me from the range, and the sun was sinking. But the worst of it all was that there were several miles of rough and strange country between me and Grand Lake that would have to be made in the dark. I did not care to take any more chances on the ice, so I spent a hard hour climbing out of the canyon. The climb warmed me and set my clothes steaming.

My watch indicated six o'clock. A fine snow was falling, and it was dark and cold. I had been exercising for twelve hours without rest, and had eaten nothing since the previous day, as I never take breakfast. I made a fire and lay down on a rock by it to relax, and also to dry my clothes. In half an hour I started on again. Rocky and forest-covered ridges lay between me and Grand Lake. In the darkness I certainly took the worst way. I met with too much resistance in the thickets and too little on the slippery places, so that when, at eleven o'clock that night, I entered a Grand Lake Hotel, my appearance was not prepossessing.

The next day, after a few snow measurements, I set off to re-cross the range. In order to avoid warm bear dens and cold streams, I took a different route. It was a much longer way than the one I had come by, so I went to a hunter's deserted cabin for the night. The cabin had no door, and I could see the stars through the roof. The old sheet-iron stove was badly rusted and broken. Most of the night I spent chopping wood, and I did not sleep at all. But I had a good rest by the stove, where I read a little from a musty pamphlet on palmistry that I found between the logs of the cabin. I always carry candles with me. When the wind is blowing, the wood damp, and the fingers numb, they are of inestimable value in kindling a fire. I do not carry firearms, and during the night, when a lion gave a blood-freezing screech, I wished he were somewhere else.

Daylight found me climbing toward the top of the range through the Medicine Bow National Forest, among some of the noblest evergreens in Colorado. When the sun came over the range, the silent forest vistas became magnificent with bright lights and deep shadows. At timberline the bald rounded summit of the range, like a gigantic white turtle, rose a thousand feet above me. The slope was steep and very icy; a gusty wind whirled me about. Climbing to the top would be like going up a steep ice covered house roof. It would be a dangerous and barely possible undertaking. But as I did not have courage enough to retreat, I threw off my snowshoes and started up. I cut a place in the ice for every step. There was nothing to hold to, and a slip meant a fatal slide.

With rushes from every quarter, the wind did its best to freeze or overturn me. My ears froze, and my fingers grew so cold that they could hardly hold the ice axe. But after an hour of constant peril and ever increasing exhaustion, I got above the last ice and stood upon the snow. The snow as solidly packed, and, leaving my snowshoes strapped across my shoulders, I went scrambling up. Near the top of the range a ledge of granite cropped out through the snow, and toward this I hurried. Before making a final spurt to the ledge, I paused to breathe. As I stopped, I was startled by sounds like the creaking of wheels on a cold, snowy street. The snow beneath me was slipping! I had started a snow-slide.

Almost instantly the slide started down the slope with me on it. The direction in which it was going and the speed it was making would in a few seconds carry it down two thousand feet of slope, where it would leap over a precipice into the woods. I was on the very upper edge of the snow that had started, and this was the tail end of the slide. I tried to stand up in the rushing snow, but its speed knocked my feet from under me, and in an instant I was rolled beneath the surface. Beneath the snow, I went tumbling on with it for what seemed like a long time, but I know, of course, that it was for only a second or two; then my feet struck against something solid. I was instantly flung to the surface again, where I either was spilled off, or else fell through, the end of the slide, and came to a stop on the scraped and frozen ground, out of the grasp of the terrible snow.

I leaped to my feet and saw the slide sweep on in most impressive magnificence. At the front end of the slide the snow piled higher and higher, while following in its wake were splendid streamers and scrolls of snow-dust. I lost no time in getting to the top, and set off southward, where, after six miles, I should come to the trail that led to my starting place on the east side of the range. After I had made about three miles, the cold clouds closed in, and everything was fogged. A chilly half-hour's wait and the clouds broke up. I had lost my ten foot staff in the snow-slide, and feeling for precipices without it would probably bring me out upon another snow cornice, so I took no chances.

I was twelve thousand five hundred feet above sea level when the clouds broke up, and from this great height I looked down upon what seemed to be the margin of the polar world. It was intensely cold, but the sun shone with dazzling glare, and the wilderness of snowy peaks came out like a grand and jagged ice field in the far south. Halos and peculiarly luminous balls floated through the color tinged and electrical air. The horizon had a touch of cobalt blue, and on the dome above, white flushes appeared and disappeared like faint auroras. After five hours on these silent but imposing heights I struck my first day's trail, and began a wild and merry coast down among the rocks and trees to my starting place.

I hope to have more winter excursions, but perhaps I have had my share. At the bare thought of those winter experiences I am again on an unsheltered peak struggling in a storm; or I am in a calm and splendid forest upon whose snowy, peaceful aisles fall the purple shadows of crags and pines.

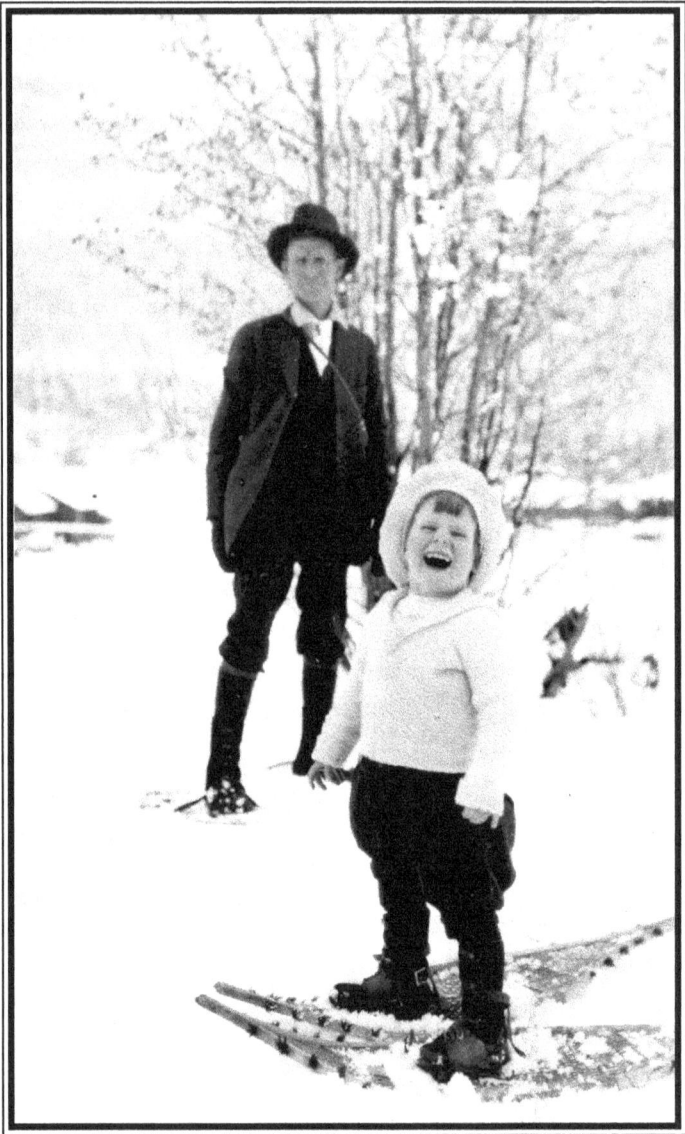

Enos and his daughter, Enda, go snowshoeing.

Far clouds of feathery gold,
Shaded with deepest purple, gleam
Like islands on a dark blue sea.
     Percy Shelley

Dweller of Mountain Tops

I was traveling the high plateau summit of the Continental Divide on snowshoes. At the top of a large snowdrift I lay down for a look through my double-barrel glasses. Only a few hundred feet away was a flock of Bighorn sheep, seventeen in all.

The sheep were snowbound in a snow-walled, countersunk depression, surrounded by snow-piled peaks. The pasture where they were feeding was more than a thousand feet above the limits of tree growth and twelve thousand feet above the surface of the sea.

A number of the sheep were playing; no sentinels were out. Their playground was small and they could see all approaches to it. These seventeen Bighorns were not worrying about enemies. On they went with play for an hour, the two young lambs leaping, rearing, and butting with vitality and enjoyment.

Ragged, grassy spaces above the treeline are found over the summits of the Rocky Mountains. These afford year round pasturage for mountain sheep. The snowfall on parts of these mountains is heavy. But each fall of snow is commonly followed by a windy day or two; often spaces, acres across, are swept nearly bare while big drifts, white hills rising from gray valleys, are piled up as snowy barriers between the dried grass moorlands.

The sheep in this skyline feeding ground probably had been there for weeks. As I turned down the mountain I realized that their small pasture was already overgrazed, practically exhausted.

The wind had swept most of the snow out of this bowl-like depression. But the life of the flock was imperilled. Even while most members were playing in temporary security, two of the older sheep were restlessly searching the edges of the surrounding snowy wall for a way of escape. There did not appear to be any way, any escape.

That night there came another heavy fall of snow. This was followed by several hours' high wind, which swept the snow off the plateau. But it did not add any more grass for the flock of sheep, and the deepened snow barrier around them might extend their sentence there. This flock, walled in by vast drifts, was facing starvation.

Ordinarily, sheep give little thought concerning the weather changes. If an advancing storm catches them down the mountain they commonly hasten to their home territory on the heights. Many times I have thought that they take shelter among those rocks that are closest to the grassy spaces first cleared of snow. And a few times I have seen flocks in deep snow on the summit eagerly looking in the direction from which the Chinook wind came hours later.

A large cliff on the slope of a nearby peak, a little above the timberline, stands humped up with its back to the northwest. This, so sign showed, had long been used by sheep as a shelter from westerly storms.

One day I crept up close to this cliff. Snow was falling and a breeze blowing from the west. When within about thirty feet of the eastern, leeward side, I could dimly see a number of sheep crowded, head outward, beneath the overhanging ledge of rock.

Later, when the snow had stopped falling, I went back. I took a look through my field glass when about five hundred feet away. There stood the sheep beneath the cliff. Scattered a little, they were enjoying the sunshine. They had been huddled here three days and nights and I suppose were now eager to eat, but getting at the short brown grass could not easily be done through three feet of snow. They were waiting for the wind to blow—for a windstorm to sweep clean the snow-buried pasture.

That night the wind blew violently. The following morning with a field glass I could see gray-brown spaces already bare of snow. The wind was still blowing. At times the air was so filled with snow-dust that the mountains were hidden. But under the lee of the skyline near their cliff shelter the sheep were feeding in the ragged cleared spaces. The wind was ripping across their feeding ground, surging sixty to eighty miles an hour. But they did not mind. They were dressed for it. Occasionally a pair rose on hind legs playfully to spar and fence with horns. Now and then one stopped feeding to rub against a boulder, or to scratch with a hind foot.

Colorado has an extensive area, an area about equal to New Jersey, that is high plateau and entirely above the limits of tree growth. This plateau, broken by canyons and peaks, is extremely rocky; it has small perpetual snow- and ice-fields and innumerable grassy meadows.

Here is the home of mountain sheep. Deer and elk use it in summer, but during the winter the Bighorn is the only hoofed animal living upon it.

The Bighorn is a mountaineer. He is in repose on a narrow ledge and enjoys steep inclines where smooth rock and icy spaces exact the highest climbing skill. A few people have expressed the view that he has but recently taken to the mountain tops because of long-range rifles and excessive hunting. Accounts left by early hunters and trappers give no conclusive facts on the matter. But his warm clothing, his indifference to wind and extreme cold, and his feet—the perfection of adjustment to rock and ice work showing ages of evolution—indicate that for generations he has been a year-round dweller of mountain tops. It would appear that sheep are living on the heights the year round because they find it a good place to live.

Snow is deadly for the elk and the deer of the lowlands where forests shelter it and prevent the winds from blowing it off, but rarely is it a menace to the sheep on the heights. Above the timberline the wind is likely to be more frequent, and also more effective as a snow sweeper or remover. Here its power, perhaps, is more often intensified than impeded by the topography.

But the snow-bound flock of seventeen on the summit was starved out. The next time I saw the sheep they were breaking a trail into a gigantic snowdrift on the south side of their prison. Evidently they knew that another pasture lay off to the south more than a mile distant. It was a larger one, and it, too, had been swept clean of snow. But just how they could make their way through and around the deep snowdrifts to reach it was incomprehensible to me.

I found shelter near by for a few nights in an abandoned mining tunnel, and during the day kept out of sight of the flock and watched it.

The first glimpse that I had of the sheep making efforts to leave their exhausted feeding ground was of a ewe rearing up on hind legs, then, with a leap upward and forward, coming down upon the snow with all her might. This she did over and over, perhaps for half an hour, when she dropped exhausted. During this half hour she had made an advance of only a few feet. But she had battered a trail into the fifteen-foot depth of snow over which the other sheep could walk. Out in the barren opening other members of the flock were lying down, standing, or playing.

When the ewe dropped exhausted a ram instantly leaped over her and continued the snow battering. Behind the ram stood another one waiting for his turn.

It was single-file trail-breaking. The deep and soft snow gave no support for small, hard feet and heavy sheep. Often only the head showed above the drift, and in a number of places even the head sank below the snow level. This snow barrier was almost as difficult to cross as a bottomless bog. The sheep, though powerful and of excellent endurance, worked under the greatest disadvantages. Now and then a hidden rock point gave the trail-breaker momentary good footing and he would leap high and come down bodily upon the snow. But altogether, progress was slow. It took from five to twelve minutes for a sheep to advance his length.

While the lead sheep was laboring to open the way, the others in single file commonly stood watching his efforts. Now and then a few lay down in the trampled trail and those behind stepped over them. Now and then the two lambs leaped upon the back of the ewe in front of them.

In places where rocks lay near the snow surface the sheep nosed about, getting a bite of grass or an alpine wild flower stalk. Midafternoon when I left them they were in line, with the ewe battering away, beating and packing a narrow, deep trail-way into the snow.

The following morning when I returned they had advanced more than one hundred feet. Their advance indicated that they must have labored all night.

Mid-morning they broke through the drift on the south side of their feeding ground and came out into a space where the snow was shallow. Here they turned abruptly to the right into the end of a gulch, wallowing forward single file. In a few minutes they had descended behind a snow cornice. I climbed to where I could see down the gulch and found that from it the wind, uprushing, had carried most of the snow.

On the left of the flock the wall was of rocks, too steep to hold snow, but sheeted with thin ice. On the right, the low, ragged gulch side was rock points and snow piles.

Late afternoon the sheep began to make their way out of the valley on a knife edge of rock which thrust from the wall on the left. Just at sunset I saw them along the bleak skyline. On the wide summit they paused to rest and all lay down except the lambs. These butted each other and leaped from back to back of the old ones.

During the night the sheep climbed a ridge to a point that connected with a plateau several hundred feet higher than, and directly south of, their old pasture. Evidently they had had to go down into the gulch to search for a way by which they could reach this summit, for immediately in front of the place where they had left their pasture there was nothing but an icy, unscalable wall.

That night they were attacked by a mountain lion. They were in deep snow up to their necks, battling a drift on the edge of the plateau. The large soft feet of the lion sank but a few inches and he thus had marked advantage over them.

Tracks told a stirring story. The lion had slipped close to the lead sheep but appears to have been discovered. Impressions in the snow showed that the lead sheep had reared up, moving from side to side as the lion watched for a chance to spring. Evidently the lion hesitated about leaping unless he could surprise or could have the sheep at a disadvantage. Back along the line, then, he edged, probably facing all the defensive horns of the sheep. Finally he leaped.

It is likely that he spent the next several minutes or days in wishing that he had not done so. Just as he sprang a sheep had reared up and struck him with its horns. But the shock was sufficient to overturn the sheep and it fell with the lion underneath.

This cut the line of sheep into two sections. Blood and the hair on the snow told that the lion had done savage clawing and biting. But he, too, was roughly handled. The sheep had butted him, trampled upon him, horned him, and rolled him over. It is likely that ribs were broken. When he finally escaped he made but three tracks in the snow. His left hind leg was out of commission.

While this fight was going on another lion appeared behind the sheep. Evidently the rear one, a ewe, had scented him and bravely gone to intercept him. She left the trail and advanced in shallow snow. Then, while she was wallowing in deeper snow, the lion had leaped upon her.

The struggle appears to have been fierce but brief. Though the force of the striking lion had jammed the ewe into the snow, she had quickly risen. The lion, to tire her, had leaped over her a few times. He easily avoided her lunges and watched for his opportunity. At last he landed upon her, knocking her upon her side. Seizing her by the throat, probably, he had dragged her to a rock outcrop a few yards away, where he had eaten his fill. He went back along his tracks made in coming to the scene.

A large, windswept, grassy space lay about a mile ahead of the sheep. But the snow barrier between seemed impassable for any large animal that did not wear snowshoes or possess large, soft, lion-like feet. This was a winter of much more than usual snowfall. There were acres of grass—enough for a thousand times as many sheep as ranged the heights, but this grass was deeply buried.

Mountain sheep normally range from one place to another. Ordinarily, these sheep could have gone to the other pasture in an hour without effort. But this winter the deeply drifted snow made movement almost impossible.

Frequently I had a good view of them through my glasses. They kept struggling forward. Much of the time I advanced parallel to them, keeping from two hundred to three hundred yards away so as not to worry them. I also watched the wind, and I do not believe they scented me.

They climbed for some distance over thin pinnacled edges, seemingly impossible to traverse. They wallowed shallow places and struggled through deep stretches.

Again they were attacked by the lions, as the snow record showed. One badly wounded in the night by the lion leaped short and fell in the deep snow between large boulders. He struggled for some time before he hooked fore hoofs over a point on a boulder and drew himself out and up, and lay down. There was blood on the snow.

Quickly a watchful animal discovers that his possible victims are in trouble. If an early snow catches beavers still harvesting, wolves and lions soon discover that the snow hampers their movements, and near the pond they wait for the chance to catch one. So it was on the heights; these lions having discovered that deep snow was hampering the movements of the sheep, watched day after day for the opportunity to seize one of the flock.

The sheep were crossing a moraine of large boulders. Keeping well apart, each easily leaped from top to top of boulders which had been swept bare of snow. A few leaped to side boulders and turned to look at the fallen one. The old ram leading did not glance back; he did sentinel duty ahead and probably planned the next advance. The two lambs became restless. Each leaped on the back of the sheep ahead of it, and there stood looking playfully this way and that, utterly unacquainted with the peril of the flock. They leaped off as all started on. Not again did any of them look back at the wounded one.

They had started for the edge of the plateau as their movement later showed. It was little more than a thousand feet to the rim, but most of this way was covered with two deep snow fields. Had the snow been packed, so as to sustain the sheep, they would have crossed in a minute.

In making this one thousand feet they must have traveled two miles. With long zigzags they dodged most of the deep snow and walked on sharp rock ridges and boulder tops. Mid-afternoon fourteen stood on the edge of the plateau where it dropped precipitously several hundred feet into a canyon.

For miles the high white tableland stretched away. It was from a half mile to a mile and a half wide. Though comparatively level, its summit combined gulches, ridges, cliffs, and rocky pinnacles. These divided the smoother slopes and the whitened grassy meadows.

The majority of the days on these heights were calm and sunny; the nights not extremely cold, with the sky full of stars. Occasionally the shadow of an eagle slid across the snow, or a little cony called from a rock near his den, or a flock of white ptarmigan walked quietly about or flew cackling away.

One of the sheep had dropped out since leaving the place where the injured one lay down. Out of my sight as they were much of the time, I had no idea where or how he had disappeared. But a count showed one fewer. As for the wounded sheep—the last look that I had of him was not pleasant. His proud head lay on the boulder, his end near. As I watched, beyond him a lion walked out on a snowy point and surveyed the scene.

From the canyon rim to which the flock had now come the possible pasture was still nearly a mile distant. But this rim, extending to within a stone's throw of it, could possibly be used as a line of advance. Stretches where the snow had caved off offered scant, though mostly secure, footing; other stretches were imperilled with snow ready to slip overboard. Single file, evenly spaced, the sheep slowly advanced.

If they ever reached the new pasture they would have traveled nearly twenty miles besides hundreds of feet up and down. Beeline this new pasture was but little more than a mile from the old one.

About a quarter of a mile beyond the starting point on the canyon's rim a rounded, snow-covered ridge arose to block the way. The sheep made this quarter of a mile in half an hour and without accident. But if they were to attempt to climb the ridge, they would have hours of work in deep snow again.

They were walking easily along on the exposed rocks. Within a stone's throw of the snowy ridge the lead ram without hesitating leaped and disappeared into the canyon. A moment later another and another followed in order. Each went over and out of sight. Evidently they had been here before. Probably they knew where they were and the way below and around the obstruction. I snowshoed forward to see if they would make it back up the canyon wall to the farther side of the ridge.

When I reached a high point two of the sheep had already come out on top. They had descended about one hundred feet and then climbed up again on narrow ledges covered with ice. All this in a few minutes. So, of course, the leader had been over this trail before.

A sharp ridge which the sheep did not even try to climb broke off near the edge of the canyon. The space between it and the precipitous rim was full of snow. Through this the sheep were forcing their way when the whole mass slipped, carrying all to the edge and one lamb and one of the older ones over. As the snow dust cleared I could see two were struggling on the rim. These finally pulled themselves up.

I started back for the cabin of the miners, but lingered on a snowdrift the other side of the grassy pasture to see if the sheep might make it that night, wondering if they could make it at all.

They had spent three days and two nights in the struggle. This in almost constant effort with almost no food, and they half starved at the starting. The last look I had of the flock showed the remaining twelve walking single file on the very edge of the precipice looking indifferently down into the depths, as they stepped or leaped forward from one perilous footing to the next.

While I waited, a lion appeared among the rocks on the snow barrier of their pasture at a point where I was expecting the sheep to appear. He waited. It was almost dark and I was about to start on when in the lower part of the windswept grassland I caught a shadowy glimpse of the sheep. Out into the open, gaunt, the eleven raced, with the little lamb leading and kick up his heels.

Enos sits at the cairn marking the top of Long's Peak.

The Great Nature in which we rest as the earth lies in the soft arms of the atmosphere.
Ralph Waldo Emerson

Mountaintop Weather

The narrow Alpine zone of peaks and snow that forms the crest of the Rocky Mountains has its own individual elemental moods, its characteristic winds, its electrical and other peculiarities, and a climate of its own. Commonly its days are serene and sunny, but from time to time it has hail and snow and showers of windblown rain, cold as ice water. It is subject to violent changes from clear, calm air to blizzard.

I have enjoyed these strange, silent heights in every season of the year. In climbing scores of these peaks, in crossing the passes, often on snowshoes, and in camping here and there on the skyline, I have encountered these climatic changes and had numerous strange experiences. From these experiences I realize that the transcontinental aviator, with this realm of peak and sky, will have some delightful as well as serious surprises. He will encounter stern conditions. He may, like a storm-defying bird, be carried from his course by treacherous currents and battle with breakers or struggle in vain in the monstrous, invisible maelstroms that beset this ocean of air. Of these skyline factors the more imposing are wind, cold, clouds, rain, snow, and subtle, capricious electricity.

High winds are common across the summits of these mountains; and they are most prevalent in winter. Those of summer, though less frequent and much more short-lived, are a menace on account of their fury and the suddenness with which they surprise and sweep the heights.

Early one summer, while exploring a wide alpine moorland above the timberline, I—and some others—had an experience with one of those sudden storm bursts. The region was utterly wild, but up to it straggling tourists occasionally rode for a view of the surrounding mountain world. All alone, I was studying the ways of the wild inhabitants of the heights. I had spent the calm, sunny morning in watching a solitary bighorn that was feeding among some boulders. He was aged, and he ate as though his teeth were poor and walked as though afflicted with rheumatism. Suddenly this patriarch forgot his age and fled precipitately, with almost the speed of frightened youth. I leaped upon a boulder to watch him, but was instantly knocked headlong by a wild blast of wind. In falling I caught sight of a straw hat and a wrecked umbrella falling out of the sky. Rising amid the pelting gale of flung hail, ice water, and snow, I pushed my way in the teeth of the storm, hoping for shelter in the lee of a rock pile about a hundred yards distant. A lady's disheveled hat blew by me, and with the howl of the wind came, almost drowned, excited human utterances. Nearing the rock pile, I caught a vague view of a merry-go-round of man and horse, then a glimpse of the last gyration, in which an elderly Eastern gentleman parted company with a stampeded bronco.

Five tourists had ridden up in the sunshine to enjoy the heights, and the suddenness and fierceness of the storm had thrown them into a panic and stampeded their horses. They were drenched and severely chilled, and they were frightened. I made haste to tell them that the storm would be brief. While I was still trying to reassure them, the clouds commenced to dissolve and the sun came out. Presently all were watching the majestic soaring of two eagles up in the blue, while I went off to collect five scattered saddle-ponies that were contentedly feeding far away on the moor.

Though the winter winds are of slower development, they are more prolonged and are tempestuously powerful. Occasionally these winds blow for days; and where they follow a fall of snow they blow and whirl this about so wildly that the air is befogged for several hundred feet above the earth. So violently and thickly is the powdered snow flung about that a few minutes at a time is the longest that one can see or breathe in it. These high winter winds come out of the west in a deep, broad stratum that is far above most of the surface over which they blow. Commonly a high wind strikes the western slope of the Continental Divide a little below the altitude of eleven thousand feet. This striking throws it into fierce confusion. It rolls whirling up the steeps and frequently shoots far above the highest peaks. Across the passes it sweeps, roars down the canyons on the eastern slope, and rushes out across the plains. Though the western slope below eleven thousand feet is a calm zone, the entire eastern slope is being whipped and scourged by a flood of wind.

Occasionally the temperature of these winds is warm.

These swift, insistent winds, torn, intercepted, and deflected by dashing against the broken skyline, produce currents, counter-currents, sleepy eddies, violent vertical whirls, and milling maelstroms that are tilted at every angle. In places there is a gale blowing upward, and here and there the air pours heavily down in an invisible but almost crushing air fall.

One winter I placed an air meter in Granite Pass, at twelve thousand feet altitude on the slope of Long's Peak. During the first high wind I fought my way up to read what the meter said. Both the meter and myself found the wind exceeded the speed limit. Emerging above the trees at timberline, I had to face the unbroken fury of the gale as it swept down the slope from the heights above. The region was barren of snow. The wind dashed me with sandblasts and pelted me with gravel volleys that were almost unbearable. My face and wrists were bruised, and blood was drawn in many places where the gravel struck.

Seeking rest and shelter from this persistent punishment, I approached a crag and when only a few yards away was struck and overturned by the milling air current around it. The air was so agitated around this crag that its churnings followed me, like disturbed water, under and behind the large rock fragments, where shelter was hoped for but only partly secured.

On the last slope below the meter the wind simply played with me. I was overthrown, tripped, knocked down, blown explosively off my feet and dropped. Sometimes the wind dropped me heavily, but just as often it eased me down. I made no attempt to stand erect; most of the time this was impossible and at all times it was very dangerous. Now and then the wind rolled me as I lay resting upon a smooth place. Advancing was akin to swimming a whirlpool or to wrestling one's way up a slope despite the ceaseless opposition of a vigorous, tireless opponent.

At last I crawled and climbed up to the buzzing cups of the meter. So swiftly were they rotating they formed a blurred circle, like a fast-revolving life preserver. The meter showed that the wind was passing with a speed of from one hundred and sixty-five to one hundred and seventy miles an hour. The meter blew up—or, rather, flew to pieces—during a swifter spurt.

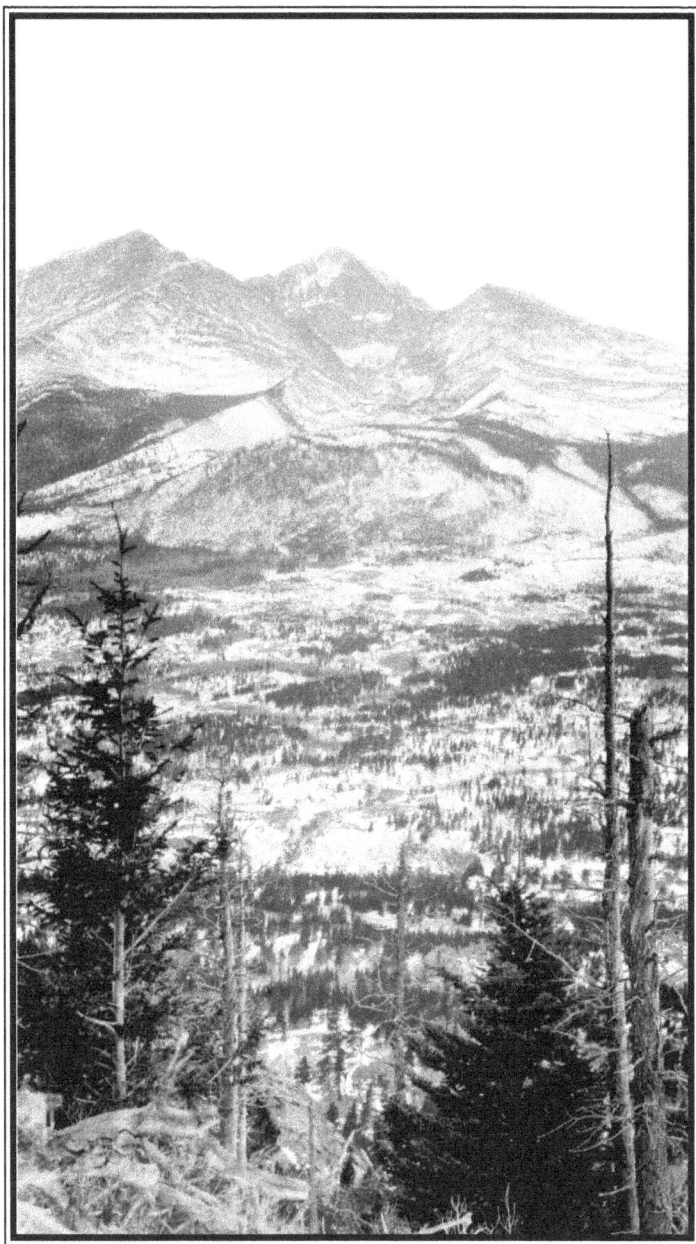

Long's Peak and Tahosa Valley,
after the 1900 forest fire.

The wind so loudly ripped and roared round the top of the peak that I determined to scale the summit and experience its wildest and most eloquent efforts. All my strength and climbing knowledge were required to prevent my being literally blown out of converging rock channels through which the wind gushed; again and again I clung with all my might to avoid being torn from the ledges. Fortunately not a bruise was received, though many times this was narrowly avoided.

The top of the peak, an area of between three and four acres and comparatively level, was in an easy eddy, almost a calm when compared with the wind's activities below and nearby. Apparently the wind current collided so forcefully with the western wall of the peak that it was thrown far above the summit before recovering to continue its way eastward; but against the resisting spurs and pinnacles a little below summit level the wind roared, boomed, and crashed in its determined, passionate onsweep.

The better to hear this grand uproar, I advanced to the western edge of the summit. Here my hat was torn off, but not quite grasped, by the upshooting blast. It fell into the swirl above the summit and in large circles floated upward at slow speed, rising directly above the top of the peak. It rose and circled so slowly that I threw several stones at it, trying to knock it down before it rose out of range. The diameter of the circle through which it floated was about one hundred and fifty feet; when it had risen five, or perhaps six, hundred feet above the summit it suddenly tumbled over and over as though about to fall, but instead of falling it sailed off toward the east as though a carrier pigeon hurrying for a known and definite place in the horizon.

Some of the gulf streams, hell gates, whirlpools, rough channels, and dangerous tides in the sea of air either are in fixed places or adjust themselves to winds from a different quarter so definitely that their location can be told by considering them in connection with the direction of the wind. Thus the sea of air may be partly charted and the position of some of its dangerous places, even in mountaintop oceans, positively known.

However, there are dangerous mountaintop winds of one kind, or, more properly, numerous local air blasts, that are sometimes created within these high winds, that do not appear to have any habits. It would be easier to tell where the next thunderbolt would fall than where the next one of these would explode. One of these might be called a cannon wind. An old prospector who had experienced countless high winds among the crags, once stated that high, gusty winds on mountain slopes "sometimes shoot off a cannon." These explosive blasts touch only a short, narrow space, but in this they are almost irresistible.

Isolated clouds often soften and beautify the stern heights as they silently float and drift among peaks and passes. Flocks of these sky birds frequently float about together. On sunny days, in addition to giving a charm to the peaks, their restless shadows never tire of readjusting themselves and are ever trying to find a foundation or a place of rest upon the tempestuous topography of the heights below. Now and then a deep, dense cloud stratum will cover the crests and envelop the summit slopes for days. These vapory strata usually feel but little wind and they vary in thickness from a few hundred to a few thousand feet. Sometimes one of these rests so serenely that it suggests an aggregation of clouds pushed off to one side because temporarily the sky does not need them elsewhere for either decorative or precipitative purpose. Now and then they do drop rain or snow, but most of the time they appear to be in a procrastinating mood and unable to decide whether to precipitate or to move on.

Commonly the upper surfaces of cloud strata appear like a peaceful silver-gray sea. They appear woolly and sometimes fluffy, level, and often so vast that they sweep away beyond the horizon. Peaks and ridges often pierce their interminable surface with romantic continents and islands; along their romantic shores, above the surface of the picturesque sea, the airship could sail in safe poetic flight, though the foggy depths below were too dense for any traveler to penetrate.

One spring the snow fell continuously around my cabin for three days. Reports told that the storm was general over the Rocky Mountain region. Later investigations showed that that cloud and storm were spread over a quarter of a million square miles. Over this entire area there was made a comparatively even deposit of thirty inches of snow.

All over the area, the bottom, or under surface, of the cloud was at an altitude of approximately nine thousand feet. My cabin, with an altitude of nine thousand, was immersed in cloud, though at times it was one hundred feet or so below it. Fully satisfied of the widespread and general nature of the storm, and convinced of the comparatively level line of the bottom surface of the cloud, I determined to measure its vertical depth and observe its slow movements by climbing above its silver lining. This was the third day of the storm. On snowshoes up the mountainside I went through this almost opaque sheep's-wool cloud. It was not bitterly cold, but cloud and snow combined were blinding, and only a ravine and instinct enabled me to make my way.

At an altitude of about twelve thousand feet the depth of the snow became suddenly less, soon falling to only an inch or so. Within a few rods of where it began to grow shallow I burst through the upper surface of the cloud. Around me and above there was not a flake of snow. Over the entire storm area of a quarter of a million square miles, all heights above twelve thousand had escaped both cloud and snow. The cloud, which thus lay between the altitudes of nine thousand and twelve thousand feet, was three thousand feet deep.

When I rose above the surface of this sea the sun was shining upon it. It was a smooth sea; not a breath of wind ruffled it. The top of Long's Peak rose bald and broken above. Climbing to the top of a commanding ridge, I long watched this beautiful expanse of cloud and could scarcely realize that it was steadily flinging multitudes of snowflakes upon slopes and snows below. Though practically stationary, this cloud expanse had some slight movements. These were somewhat akin to those of a huge raft that it becalmed in a quiet harbor. Slowly, easily, and almost imperceptibly the entire mass slid forward along the mountains; it moved but a short distance, paused for some minutes, then slowly slid back a trifle farther than it had advanced. After a brief stop the entire mass, as though anchored in the center, started to swing in an easy, deliberate rotation; after a few degrees of movement it paused, hesitated, then swung with slow, heavy movement back. In addition to these shifting horizontal motions there was a short vertical one. The entire mass slowly sank and settled two or three hundred feet, then, with scarcely a pause, rose easily to the level from which it sank. Only once did it rise above this level.

During all seasons of the year there are oft-recurring periods when the mountains sit in sunshine and all the winds are still. In days of this kind of transcontinental passengers in glass-bottomed airships would have a bird's-eye view of sublime scenes. The purple forests, the embowered, peaceful parks, the drifted snows, the streams that fold and shine through the forests,—all these combine and cover magnificently the billowed and broken distances, while ever floating up from below are the soft, ebbing, and intermittent songs from white water that leaps in glory.

Though the summits of the Rocky Mountains are always cool, it is only in rare, brief times that they fall within the frigid spell of Farthest North and become cruelly cold. The climate among these mountaintops is much milder than people far away imagine.

The electrical effects that enliven and sometimes illuminate these summits are peculiar and often highly interesting. Thunderbolts—lighting strokes—are rare, far less frequent than in most lowland districts. However, when lightning does strike the heights, it appears to have many times the force that is displayed in lowland strokes. My conclusions concerning the infrequency of thunderbolts on these sky-piercing peaks are drawn chiefly from my own experience. I have stood through storms upon more than a score of Rocky Mountain summits that were upward of fourteen thousand feet above the tides. Only one of these peaks was struck; this was Long's Peak, which rises to the height of 14,256 feet above the sea.

Seventy storms I have experienced on the summit of this peak, and during these it was struck but three times to my knowledge. One of these strokes fell a thousand feet below the top; two struck the same spot on the edge of the summit. The rock struck was granite, and the effects of the strokes were similar; hundreds of pounds of shattered rock fragments were flung horizontally afar. Out of scores of experiences in rain-drenched passes I have record of but two thunderbolts. Both of these were heavy. In all these instances the thunderbolt descended at a time when the storm cloud was a few hundred feet above the place struck.

During the greater number of high altitude storms the cloud is in contact with the surface or but little removed from it. Never have I known the lightning to strike when the clouds were close to the surface or touching it. It is, however, common, during times of low dragging clouds, for the surface air to be heavily charged with electrical fluid. This often is accompanied with strange effects. Prominent among these is a low pulsating hum or an intermittent *buz-z-z-z*, with now and then a sharp *zit-zit!* Sometimes accompanying, at other times only briefly breaking in, are subdued campfire cracklings and roarings. Falling snowflakes, during these times, are occasionally briefly luminous, like fireflies, the instant they touch the earth. Hair-pulling is the commonest effect that people experience in these sizzling electrical storms. There is a straightening of the hairs and apparently a sharp pull upon each. As John Muir has it, "You are sure to be lost in wonder and praise and every hair of your head will stand up and hum and sing like an enthusiastic congregation." Most people take very gravely their first experience of this kind; especially when accompanied, as it often is, with apparent nearby bee-buzzings and a purplish roll or halo around the head. During these times a sudden finger movement will produce a crackling snap or spark.

On rare occasions these interesting peculiarities become irritating and sometimes serious to one. In "A Watcher on the Heights" in *Wild Life on the Rockies*, I have described a case of this kind. A few people suffer from a muscular cramp or spasm, and occasionally the muscles are so tensed that breathing becomes difficult and heart action disturbed. I have never known an electrical storm to be fatal. Relief from the effects of such a storm may generally be had by lying between big stones or beneath shelving rocks. On one occasion I saw two ladies and four gentlemen lay dignity aside and obtain relief by jamming into a place barely large enough for two. In my own case, activity invariably intensified these effects; and the touching of steel or iron often had the same results. For some years a family resided upon the slope of Mt. Teller, at an altitude of twelve thousand feet. Commonly during storms the stove and pipe were charged with fluid so heavily that it was a case of hands off and let dinner wait, and sometimes spoil, until the heavens shut off the current.

The sustaining buoyancy of the air to aerial things decreases with altitude. In this "light" air some motor machinery is less efficient than it is in the lowlands. It is probable that aviators will always find the air around uplifted peaks much less serviceable than this element upon the surface of the sea. But known and unknown dangers in the air will be mastered, and ere long the dangers to those who take flight through the air will be no greater than the dangers to those who go down to the sea in ships. Flying across the crest of the continent, above the crags and canyons, will be enchanting, and this journey through the upper air may bring to many the first stirring message from the rocks and templed hills.

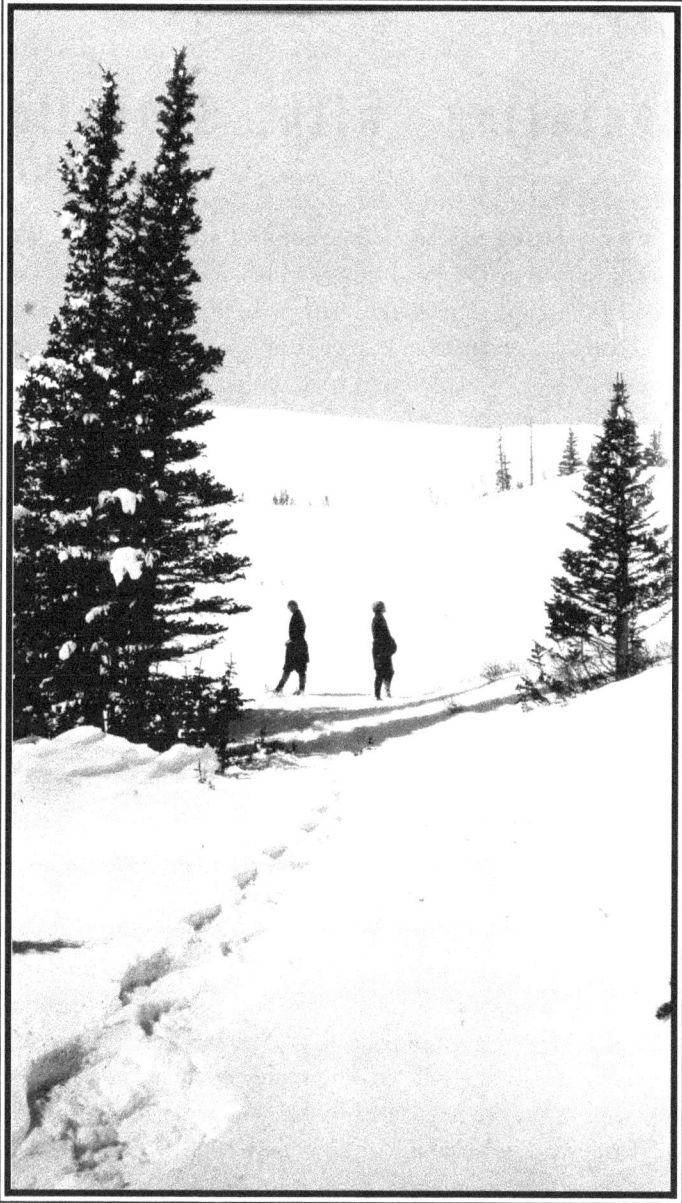

Esther Burnell Mills and Elizabeth Burnell
snowshoe near the mountaintops.

They are crystals that perish, flowers that fall.
  John Burroughs

Associating with Snowslides

Every snowfall caused a snow slide to rush down Bobtail Gulch. This runoff of snow was as regular as the runoff of storm water. The snow which accumulated at the head of this gulch was a danger to the trail below, and if the snow showed the slightest hesitation to "run" when the storm had ended, a miner from a neighboring mine started it by rolling a few stones into it or by exploding a stick of dynamite nearby.

During my stay at a miners' boarding house in the San Juan Mountains a heavy snowfall came to a close. "Has the Greagory run yet?" inquired the foreman of one of the miners. "No." "Better start it, then." Ten minutes later fifty thousand tons of snow went plunging down Greagory Gulch.

"This cabin will never be caught by a snow slide!" said the prospector with whom I was having supper. "A slide hit my cabin in the Sawtooth Mountains. No more sleeping for me in the possible right-of-way of a slide! I sized up the territory before building this cabin and I've put it out of the range of slides."

All this was encouraging, as I was to spend the night in the cabin and had arrived after the surrounding mountains were hidden in darkness. A record breaking snow of eight days and nights had just ended a few hours before. During the afternoon, as I came down from Alpine Pass on snowshoes, the visible peaks and slopes loomed white and were threateningly overladen with snow. Avalanches would run riot during the next few hours, and the sliding might begin at any minute. Gorges and old slide ways would hold most of these in the beaten slide tracks, but there was the possibility of an overladen mountain sending off a shooting star of a slide which might raise havoc by smashing open a new orbit.

The large spruces around the cabin showed that if ever a slide had swept this site it was longer ago than a century. As no steep slope came down upon the few acres of flat surrounding the cabin, we appeared to be in a slide-proof situation. However, to the north was a high snow-piled peak that did not look assuring, even though between it and the cabin was a gorge and nearby a rocky ridge. Somewhat acquainted with the ways of slides, I lay awake in the cabin, waiting to hear the muffled thunder storm of sound which would proclaim that slides were "running."

Snow slides may be said to have habits. Like water, they are governed by gravity. Both in gulches and on mountainsides, they start most readily on steep and comparatively smooth slopes. If a snowdrift is upon a thirty-degree incline, it may almost be pushed into sliding with a feather. A slope more steeply inclined than thirty degrees does not offer a snowdrift any visible means of support. Unless this slope be broken or rough, a snowdrift may slide off at any moment.

In the course of a winter, as many as half a dozen slides may start from the same place and each shoot down through the same gorge or over the same slope as its predecessor. Only so much snow can cling to a slope; therefore the number of slides during each winter is determined by the quantity of snow and the character of the slope. As soon as snow is piled beyond the holding limit, away starts the slide. A slide may have slipped from this spot only a few days before, and here another may slip away a few days later; or a year may elapse before another runs. Thus local topography and local weather conditions determine local slide habits, —when a slide will start and the course over which it will run.

The prospector was snoring before the first far-off thunder was heard. Things were moving. Seashore storm sounds could be heard in the background of heavy rumbling. This thunder swelled louder until there was a heavy rumble everywhere. Then came an earthquake jar, closely followed by a violently explosive crash. A slide was upon us! A few seconds later tons of snow fell about us, crushing the trees and wrecking the cabin. Though we escaped without a scratch, a heavy spruce pole, a harpoon flung by the slide, struck the cabin at an angle, piercing the roof and one of the walls.

The prospector was not frightened, but he was mad! Outwitted by a snow slide! That we were alive as no consolation to him. "Where on earth did the thing come from?" he kept repeating until daylight. Next morning we saw that to the depth of several feet about the cabin and on top of it were snow masses, mixed with rock fragments, broken tree trunks, and huge wood splinters,—the fragment remains of a snow slide.

This slide had started from a high peak-top a mile to the north of the cabin. For three quarters of a mile it had coasted down a slope at the bottom of which a gorge curved away toward the west; but so vast was the quantity of snow that this slide filled and blocked the gorge with less than half of its mass. Over the snowy bridge thus formed, the momentum carried the remainder straight across the gulch. Landing, it swept up a steep slope for three hundred feet and rammed the rocky ridge back of the cabin. The greater part came to a stop and lay scattered about the ridge. Not one tenth of the original bulk went over and up to the wreck of the cabin! The prospector stood on this ridge, surveying the scene and thinking, when I last looked back.

Heavy slides sometimes rush so swiftly down steep slopes that their momentum carries their entire mass destructively several hundred feet up the slope of the mountain opposite.

Desiring fuller knowledge of the birth and behavior of avalanches, or snow slides, I invaded the slide zone on snowshoes at the close of a winter which had the "deepest snow fall on record." Several days were spent watching the snow slide action in the San Juan Mountains. It was a wild, adventurous, dramatic experience, which closed with an avalanche that took me from the heights of a thrilling, spectacular coast down a steep mountain side.

A thick, snowy, marble stratum overlay the slopes and summits. Appearing on the scene at the time when, on the steeps, spring was melting the icy cement that held winter's wind-piled snows, I saw many a snowy hill and embankment released. Some of these, as slides, made meteoric plunges from summit crags to gentler places far below.

A snow storm prevailed during my first night in the slide region, and this made a deposit of five or six inches of new snow on top of the old. On the steeper places this promptly slipped off in dry, small slides, but most of it was still in place when I started to climb higher.

While I was tacking up a comparatively smooth slope, one of my snowshoes slipped and, in scraping across the old, crusted snow, started a sheaf of the fluffy new snow to slipping. Hesitatingly at first, the new snow skinned off. Suddenly the fresh snow to right and left concluded to go along, and the full width of the slope below my level was moving and creaking; slowly the whole slid into swifter movement and the mass deepened with the advance. Now and then parts of the sliding snow slide forward over the slower moving, crumpling, friction-resisted front and bottom.

With advance it grew steadily deeper from constantly acquired material and from the influence of converging water-channels which it followed. A quarter of a mile from its birthplace it was about fifty feet deep and twice as wide, with a length of three hundred feet. Composed of new snow and coasting as swiftly as a gale, it trailed a white streamer of snow-dust behind. A steeper or a rougher channel added to the volume of snow-dust or increased the agitation of the pace-keeping pennant. The morning was clear, and by watching the wig-wagging snow flag, I followed easily the fortunes of the slide to the bottom of the slope. After a swift mile of shooting and plunging, the slide, greatly compressed, sprawled and spread out over a level glacier meadow, where its last remnant lingered for the warmth of July.

Dismissing this slide, I watched along the range to the north and south, and from time to time saw the white scudding plumes of other slides, which, hidden in canyons, were merrily coasting down from the steep-sloping crest.

These slides, unless they had run down an animal, did no damage. They were composed of freshly fallen snow and in their flight had moved in old channels that had been followed and perhaps formed by hundreds of slides in years gone by. Slides of this kind—those which accompany or follow each storm and which promptly make away with new-fallen snow by carrying it down through stream channels—may be called Storm, or Flood, slides. These usually are formed in smooth gulches or on steep slopes.

The other kinds of slides may be called the Annual and the Century. In places of rough surface or moderate slope there must be a large accumulation of snow before a slide will start. Weeks or even months may pass before storm and wind assemble sufficient snow for a slide. Places of this kind commonly furnish but one slide a year, and this one in the springtime. At last the snowdrifts reach their maximum; warmth assists starting by melting snow cornices that have held on through the winter; these drop, and by dropping often start things going. Crags wedged off by winter ice are also released in spring; and these, in going recklessly down, often knock hesitating snowdrifts into action. A fitting name for those slides that regularly run at the close of winter would be Spring, or Annual. These are composed of the winter's local accumulation of snow and slide rock, and carry a much heavier percentage of rock debris than the Storm slide carries. They transport from the starting place much of the annual crumbling and the weatherings of air and water, along with the tribute pried off by winter's ice levers; with this material from the heights also goes the year's channel accumulation of debris. The Annual slide does man but little damage and, like the Flood slide, it follows the gulches and the water courses.

In snowy zones the avalanche is commonly called a snow slide, or simply a slide. A slide, with its comet tail of powdered snow, makes an intense impression on all who see one. It appears out of order with the scheme of things; but, as a matter of fact, it is one of gravity's working ways, a demonstration of the laws of sliding bodies. A smooth, steep slope which receives a heavy fall of snow will promptly produce or throw off a sliding mass of snow. Raise, lower, or roughen this slope, increase or decrease the annual snow fall, or change the direction of the wind,—and thus the position of snowdrifts,—and there will follow corresponding slide action. Wind and calm, gravity, friction, adhesion, cohesion, geology, temperature and precipitation, all have a part and place in snow-piling and in slide-starting.

The Century slides are the damaging ones. These occur not only at unexpected times but in unexpected places. The Century slide is the deadly one. It usually comes down a course not before traversed by a slide, and sometimes crashes through a forest or a village. It may be produced by a record breaking snow or by snowdrifts formed in new places by winds from an unusual quarter; but commonly the mass is of material slowly accumulated. This may contain the remnant snows and the wreckage spoils of a hundred years or more. Ten thousand snows have added to its slowly growing pile; tons of rock dust have been swept into it by the winds; gravel has been deposited in it by water; and gravity has conducted to it the crumbling rocks from above. At last—largely ice—it breaks away. In rushing down, it gathers material from its predestined way.

In the spring of 1901, one of these slides broke loose and came down the slope of Gray's Peak. For years the snow had accumulated on a ridge above timberline. The mass shot down a steep slope, struck the woods, and swept to the bottom about four thousand feet below, mowing down every tree in a pathway about three hundred feet wide. About one hundred thousand trees were piled in wild, broken wreckage in the gorge below.

Although a snow-slide is almost irresistible, it is not difficult, in many localities, to prevent slides by anchoring the small snowdrift which would slip and start the slide. In the West, a number of slides have been suppressed by setting a few posts in the upper reaches of slopes and gulches. These posts pinned fast the snow that would slip. The remainder held its own. The Swiss, too, have eliminated many Alpine slides by planting hardy shrubbery in the slippery snowy areas. This anchorage gives the snow a hold until it can compact and freeze fast. Shrubbery thus is preventing the white avalanche!

A slide once took me with it. I was near the bottom of one snowy arm of a V gulch, waiting to watch Gravity, the world-leveler, take his next fragment of filling to the lowlands. Separating these arms was a low, tongue-like rock ledge. A gigantic snow cornice and a great snow field filled, with full-heaped and rounded measure, the uppermost parts of the other arm.

Deep rumblings through the earth, echoings from crags and canyons through the communicative air, suddenly heralded the triumphant starting of an enormous slide. About three hundred feet up the heights, a broken end on embankment of rocks and snow, it came coasting, dusting into view, plunging towards me. As a rock ledge separated the two ravines above the junction, I felt secure, and I did not realize until too late that I was to coast down on the slide. Head-on, it rumbled heavily toward me with its mixed and crumbling front, making a most impressive riot of moving matter. Again and again the snowy monster smashed its shoulder into the impregnable farther wall. At last, one hundred feet high and twice as wide, came its impinging, crumbling front. At times the bottom caught and rolled under, leaving the overhanging front to cave and tumble forward with snowy splashes.

This crumbling front was not all snow; occasionally an iceberg or a cargo of stones fell forward. With snow flying from it as from a gale-swept, snow-piled summit, this monster of half a million tons roared and thundered by in a sound burst and reverberation of incomparable depth and resonance, to plunge into a deeper, steeper rock-walled gorge. It probably was moving thirty-five or forty miles an hour and was gaining velocity every second.

The noise of its passing suppressed the sounds of the slide that started in the gulch above me. Before I could realize it, this slide swept down, and the snow on which I was standing burst up with me into the air, struck and leaped the low ledge, rammed the rear end of the passing slide, and landed me, snowshoes down, on top of it.

The top was unstable and dangerous; it lurched, burst up, curled under, yawned, and gave off hissing jets of snow powder; these and the plunging movements kept me desperately active, even with my broad snowshoes, to avoid being swallowed up, or overturned and smothered, or crushed in the chaotic, fissuring mass.

As its speed increased, I now and then caught a glimpse, through flying, pelting snow particles, of shooting rocks with burst explosively through the top. At timberline the gorge walls abruptly ended and the channel curved swiftly to the left in a broad, shallow ravine. The momentum of this monster carried it out of the ravine and straight ahead over a rough, forested ridge.

Trees before it were crushed down, and those alongside were thrown into a wild state of excitement by the violence of swiftly created and entangling gale-currents. From the maelstrom on the top I looked down upon the panic through the snow-dust-filled air and saw trees flinging their arms wildly about, bowing and posturing to the snow. Occasionally a treetop was snapped off, and these broken tops swirled wildly about, hurried forward or backward, or were floated upward on rotating, slower currents. The sides of the slide crumbled and expanded; so it became lower, flatter, and wider, as it slid forward on a moderate up grade. A half mile after leaving the gorge, the slide collided at right angles with a high moraine. The stop telescoped the slide, and the shock exploded the rear third and flung it far to right and left, scattering it over a wide area. Half a minute later I clawed out of the snow pile, almost suffocated, but unhurt.

Toward the close of my last winter as government "Snow Observer"

I made a snowshoe trip along the upper slopes of the Continental Divide and scaled a number of peaks in the Rocky Mountains of central Colorado. During this trip I saw a large and impressive snow-slide at a thrillingly close range. It broke loose and "ran"—more correctly, plunged—by me down a frightful slope. Everything before it was overwhelmed and swept down. At the bottom of the slope it leaped in fierce confusion from the top of a precipice down into a canyon.

For years this snowy mass had accumulated upon the heights. It was one of the "eternal snows" that showed in summer to people far below and far away. A century of winters had contributed snows to its pile. A white hill it was in the upper slope of a gulch, where it clung, pierced and anchored by granite pinnacles. Its icy base, like poured molten lead, had covered and filled all the inequalities of the foundation upon which it rested. Time and its tools, together with its own height and weight, at last combined to release it to the clutch and eternal pull of gravity. The expanding, shearing, breaking force of forming ice, the constant cutting of emery-edged running water, and the undermining thaw of spring sent thundering downward with ten thousand varying echoes a half million tons of snow, ice, and stones.

Head-on the vast mass came exploding toward me. Wildly it threw off masses of snowy spray and agitated, confused whirlwinds of snow dust. I was watching from the top of a precipice. Below, the wide, deep canyon was filled with fleecy clouds,—a bay from a sea of clouds beyond. The slide shot straight for the cloud-filled abyss and took with it several hundred broken trees from an alpine grove that it wrecked just above the precipice.

This swift-moving monster disturbed the air, and excited, stampeding, and cyclonic winds flung me headlong as it tore by with rush and roar. I arose in time to see the entire wreckage deflected a few degrees upward as it shot far out over the cloud-made bay of the ocean. A rioting acre of rock fragments, broken trees, shattered icebergs, and masses of dusting snow hesitated momentarily in the air, then, separating, they fell whirling, hurtling, and scattering, with varying velocities,—rocks, splintered trees, and snow,—in silent flight to plunge into the white bay beneath. No sound was given forth as they fell into, and disappeared beneath, the agitated sea of clouds. How strange this noiseless fall was! A few seconds later, as the wreckage reached the bottom, there came from beneath the silent surface the muffled sounds of crash and conflict.

A locomotive plows through a
long snowdrift above timberline.

12 000 feet above the Sea
Above the Timberline
in Winter

Enos A. Mills

Every action is measured by the depth of the sentiment from which it proceeds.
    Ralph Waldo Emerson

The Colony in Winter

In the Medicine Bow Mountains one December day, I came upon a beaver house that was surrounded by a pack of wolves. These beasts were trying to break into the house. Apparently an early autumn snow had blanketed the house and thus prevented its walls from freezing. The soft condition of the walls, along with the extreme hunger of the wolves, led to this assault. Two of these animals were near the top of the house clawing away at a rapid rate. Now and then one of the sticks or poles in the house wall was encountered, and at this the wolf would bite and tear furiously. Occasionally one of the wolves caught a resisting stick in his teeth, and, leaning back, shook his head, endeavoring with all his might tear it out. A number of wolves lay about expectant; a few sat up eagerly on haunches, while others moved about snarling, driving the others off a few yards, to be in turn driven off themselves. Shortly before they discovered me, there was a fierce fight on top of the house, in which several mixed.

Even though they had broken into the house, it would have availed them nothing, for in this, as in all old colonies, there were safety tunnels from the house which extended beneath the pond to points on shore. In these tunnels the beaver find safety, if by any means the house is ruined. Although carnivorous animals are fond of beaver flesh, they rarely take the useless trouble of digging into a house. Occasionally a wolverine or a bear may dig into a thin-walled house or one not frozen, then, after breaking in, lie in weight, and endeavor to make a capture while the beaver are repairing the hole. Beaver are more secure from enemies during the winter than at any other time. It is while felling a tree far from the water or while following a shallow stream that most beaver are captured by their enemies.

Many a time in winter I have made a pleasant visit to a beaver colony. One day, a few hours after a heavy snowfall, I came out of a dark forest and stood for a time on the edge of the snow-covered pond. Around were the firs and spruces of the forest, moveless as statues and each a pointed cone of snow. Around the small snowy plain of the pond, the drooping snow-entangled willows held their heads together in contented and thoughtful silence. Everything was serene.

A clean fox track led from the woods in a straight line across the snowy surface of the pond to the house, which stood near the center of this smooth white opening. The tracks encircled the house and ascended to the top of it, where the record imprinted in the snow told that here he watchfully rested. Descending, he had sniffed at the bushy tips of the winter food pile that thrust up through the ice, then crossed the dam to plunge into the snowy tangle of willows.

Water was still pouring and gurgling down a steep beaver slide. This was ice- and snow-covered except at two points where the swift splashing water dashed intermittently from a deep icy vent. While I was examining the beauty of the up-building icy buttresses by one of the vents, a water ouzel came forth and alighted almost within reach. I stood still. After giving a few of his nodding bows, he reentered the vent. Presently he emerged from the lower vent and, alighting upon an ice-coated boulder, indifferent to the gray sky from which scattered flakes were slowly falling and despite a temperature of five below zero, he sang low and sweetly for several seconds.

Beaver do not surrender themselves to the confines of a house and pond until cold solidly covers the pond with a roof of ice. The time of this is commonly about the first of December, but the date is of course, in a measure, dependent upon latitude, altitude, and the peculiar weather conditions of each year. Most beaver return to the old colony, or start a new one by the first of September. They have had a merry rambling summer and energetically take hold to have the house and dam ready and a harvest stored by the time winter begins.

But they are not always ready. Enemies may harass them, low water delay them, or an unusually early winter or even a heavy snow may so hamper them that, despite greatest effort, the ice puts a time lock upon the pond and closes them in for the winter without sufficient supplies.

Early one October an early snowfall worked hardship in several colonies near my home. Fortunately the ponds were not deeply frozen, and those colonies which had aspen groves close to the water succeeded in felling and dragging in sufficient food supplies for the winter. As snow drifted into the groves, many of the trees harvested were cut from the tops of snow drifts, and thus left high stumps. The following summer a number of these stood for feet above the earth and presented a striking appearance alongside the 16-inch stumps of normal height.

One of these storm-caught colonies fared badly. The inhabitants were obliged to go a long distance from the water for trees, and their all too scanty harvest was gathered with some loss of life. Apparently both wolves and lions discovered the unfortunate predicament of the harvesters, and lay in wait to catch them as they floundered slowly through the snow. The following winter these colonists tunneled through the bottom—perhaps the least frozen part of the dam—and came forth for food long before the break-up of the ice. The water drained from the pond, and after the ice had melted, the bottom of the pond revealed a torn-up condition as though the starving winter inmates had dug out for food every root and root stock to be found in the bottom.

While visiting ponds at the beginning of winter, I have many times noticed that, shortly after the pond was solidly frozen over, a hole was made through the dam just below the water surface of the pond. This lowered the water level two inches or more. Did this slight lowering of the water have to do with the ventilation of the ice-covered pond, or was it to put a check on deep freezing, or for both purposes?

In the majority of cases these holes were made from ponds which, during the winter, received but a meager inflow of fresh water. Naturally, ponds receiving a strong inflow of water would be better ventilated, and would freeze less swiftly and deeply than those whose waters became stagnant. This drawing off of water after a few inches of ice had formed, would, in some places, despite the settling of the ice, form an air blanket that would delay freezing, and thus possibly prevent the ice from forming so thickly. The air admitted by drawing off the water would be inclosed beneath the ice, and might thus be helpful to the beaver inclosed in house and pond. In only a few cases were these holes made from ponds which had subway tunnels,—tunnels which run from alongside the house through the bottom of the pond to a point above water level on the shore. In a few instances the beaver, I do not know how many, came out of this hole, cut and ate a few twigs, and then returned and closed it. Twice this is used as a way out by beaver who emerged and went to other colonies. In one case the beaver entered the other pond by making a hole through the dam. In the other they entered the pond through a subway tunnel. While these holes which lower the pond level may have chiefly to do with ventilation, or may be for the purpose of putting a check on freezing, my evidence is not ample enough for final conclusions.

A sentence of close confinement for about a third of the year for an animal that breathes air and uses pure water, is simply one of the strange ways that work out with nature. While winter lasts, a beaver must spend his time either in the dark, ill-ventilated house or in the water of the pond. Apparently he does much sleeping and possibly has a dull time of it. No news, no visitors, and apparently nothing to do! Still a beaver has food, and when dangers surround the wild folk outside the pond's roof of glass, he would be considered a good risk for life insurance.

Although the pond is commonly covered with snow, or the ice curtained with air bubbles, there have been numerous times during which I have had clear views into the water, and could see and enjoy all that was going on within, as completely as though looking at fish or turtles through the glass walls of an aquarium. Often I have peered through the ice which covered the most used place of a winter beaver pond, —the area between the house entrance and the food pile. The thinness of the ice over this place was maintained by spring water which came up through the bottom, and the beaver had so arranged their affairs that they made the best use of this shallow freezing water. Of course most ponds are without springs.

Many a time I have seen a beaver come out of the doorway of his house and go swimming toward the food pile with his hands against his breast. At the pile, if there was nothing small or short enough, he set to work and gnawed it off. The piece secured was taken into the doorway either in his hands or in his teeth. Afterward a beaver—the same one, I suppose—came out of the doorway, and cast the clean bone of the stick, from which the bark had been eaten, into the bottom of the pond.

When there is nothing else to do, the beaver apparently comes into the pond a few times each day for a swim. In the midst of swimming he rises at times to the under surface of the ice and, with his nose against it, exhales a quantity of air. After remaining with nose at this point a few seconds, the action of the air bubbles indicates that he is inhaling the

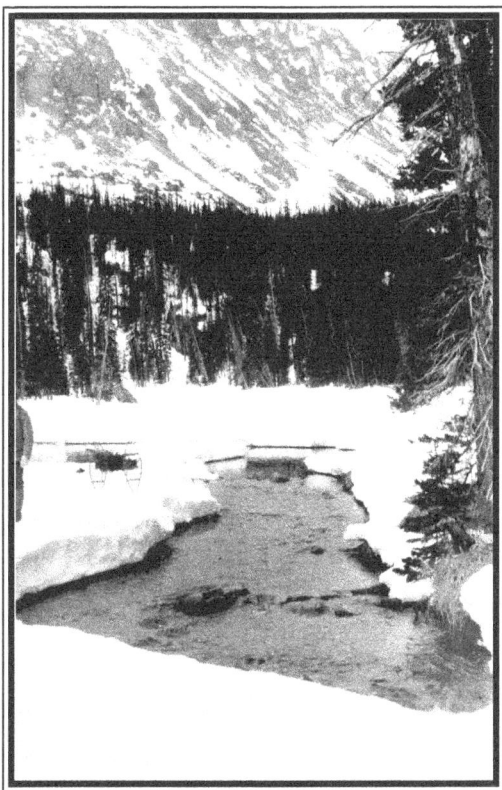

Enos snowshoes
around a partially
frozen alpine
lake affected
by beavers.

purified air.

The rootstocks of the water lily are sometimes dug from the bottom of the pond. At other times the beaver eats the stalks of plants that grow in the water, or digs out willow or other roots around the edge of the pond. Numbers of trout frequently lie in the water close to the doorway of a beaver house or around the food pile. Possibly the beaver dispense tidbits of food that are liked by the trout. Occasionally grubs fall from the holes in wood from which beaver have eaten the bark. While beaver are digging in the bottom of the pond they doubtless unearth food scraps that are welcome to trout, for these often hover in numbers on the outskirts of the muddy water which beaver roil while digging.

Although it appears that beaver have dull winters with but little to do but eat, sleep, and swim, it is probable that some of their time is spent at work. A part of their tunneling and pond bottom canal digging is done in winter. I have known of their extending canals in the bottom of the pond and making submarine tunnels while the pond was ice covered.

There are times when the dam has sprung a leak and must be repaired on the inside beneath the ice. Early thaws and spring freshets sometimes wreck a dam beyond repair, or do extensive damage to the house or dam at the time when beaver enemies are likely to be at their leanest. The house and dam are sometimes ruined when the streams are so low and icy that it is not safe for beaver to go about. I know of two colonies that were crushed out off existence by snowslides.

The dam is on rare occasions broken by late spring ice jams. Sometimes the ice cakes pile up on the dam and raise the water in the pond to such a height that it rises in the house and drives the beaver forth. A few beaver houses that are situated in places where the ice or spring floods may raise the water much above normal level are shaped to meet this trouble. The house is built higher and the room internally is twice the usual height. Thus there is a space for the beaver to build a "platform bed" on the floor and thus raise themselves a foot or more above the common level. Despite all pains, floods sometimes drive beaver to the housetops.

By laying up supplies, and by the help of artificial pond, canal, and house, the beaver is able to spend his winter without hunger and with comfort and far greater safety than his neighbors. The winds may blow and blinding snow or flying limbs may endanger those outside; snow may bury the forage of bird and deer, and make the movement of beasts of prey slow and difficult; the cold may freeze and freeze and strew the wilds with lean and frozen forms; but the beaver beneath the ice and snow shelter serenely spends the days with comfort and safety.

The winter, with its days long or short, never comes to an end, however, quite early enough to suit the beaver. They emerge from the pond at the earliest moment that frozen conditions will allow. If their subway is choked with ice, and food becomes exhausted, they will sometimes bore holes through the base of the dam.

Apparently, too, holes of this kind are bored through, or a section cut through the dam to the bottom, for the purpose of completely draining the pond. As this appears to be most often done with ponds that are full of stagnant water, or water almost stagnant, this draining by be a part of the beaver's sanitary work,—done for the purpose of getting filth and stale water out and also that the sour bottom may be sterilized by sun and wind.

Conditions determine the length of time before the dam is repaired and the pond refilled. In some cases this is done after the lapse of a few weeks and in others not until autumn. Ponds that have large pure streams running through them do not need this emptying, but occasionally they accidentally have it. Most beaver colonies are deserted in summer, and fall thus into temporary decline.

By late summer or early autumn the beaver have assembled at the place where the winter is to be spent. There are patriarchs, youngsters, and those in the prime of life. Around the old home are many who set forth from it when the violets were blooming, when the grass was at its greenest, and when mated birds were building. During the summer a few perished, while others cast their lot with other established colonies. A few of the younger make a start for themselves in new scenes,—found a new colony. Again the dam is repaired and the house recovered; again the harvest home, and again a primitive home-building family are housed in a hut that willing hands have fashioned. Again the pond freezes, and again the snow falls upon a home that stands in a valley where countless generations of beaver have lived through ice-bound winters and the ever changing happy seasons.

It is always sunrise somewhere.
  John Muir

In a Mountain Blizzard

At the close of one of our winter trips, my collie Scotch and I started across the continental divide of the Rocky Mountains in the face of weather conditions that indicated a snowstorm or a blizzard before we could gain the other side. We had eaten the last of our food twenty-four hours before and could no longer wait for fair weather. So off we started to scale the snowy steeps of the cold, gray heights a thousand feet above. The mountains already were deeply snow-covered and it would have been a hard trip even without the discomforts and dangers of a storm.

I was on snowshoes and for a week we had been camping and tramping through the snowy forests and glacier meadows at the source of the Grand River, two miles above the sea. The primeval Rocky Mountain forests are just as near to Nature's heart in winter as in summer. I had found so much to study and enjoy that the long distance from a food supply, even when the last mouthful was eaten, had not aroused me to the seriousness of the situation. Scotch had not complained, and appeared to have the keenest collie interest in the tracks and trails, the scenes and silences away from the haunts of man. The snow law seven feet deep, but by keeping in my snowshoe tracks Scotch easily followed me about. Our last camp was in the depths of an alpine forest at an altitude of ten thousand feet. Here, though zero weather prevailed, we were easily comfortable beside a fire under the protection of an overhanging cliff.

After a walk through woods the sun came blazing in our faces past snow-piled crags of Long's Peak, and threw slender blue shadows of the spiry spruces far out in a white glacier meadow to meet us. Reentering the tall but open woods, we saw, down the long aisles and limb-arched avenues, a forest of tree columns, entangled in sunlight and shadow, standing on a snowy marble floor.

We were on the Pacific slope, and our plan was to cross the summit by the shortest way between timberline and timberline on the Atlantic side. This meant ascending a thousand feet, descending an equal distance, traveling five miles amid bleak, rugged environment. Along the treeless, gradual ascent we started, realizing that the last steep ice climb would be dangerous and defiant. Most of the snow had slid from the steeper places, and much of the remainder had blown away. Over the unsheltered whole the wind was howling. For a time the sun shone dimly through the wind-driven snow dust that rolled from the top of the range, but it disappeared early behind wild, windswept clouds.

After gaining a thousand feet of altitude through the friendly forest, we climbed out and up above the trees on a steep slope at timberline. This place, the farthest up for trees, was a picturesque, desolate place. The dwarfed, gnarled, storm-shaped trees amid enormous snowdrifts told of endless, and at times deadly, struggles of the trees with the elements. Most of the trees were buried, but here and there a leaning or a storm-distorted one bent bravely above the snows.

At last we were safely on a ridge and started merrily off, hoping to cover speedily the three miles of comparatively level plateau.

How the wind did blow! Up more than eleven thousand feet above the sea, with not a tree to steady or break, it had a royal sweep. The wind appeared to be putting forth its wildest efforts to blow us off the ridge. There being a broad way, I kept well from the edges. The wind came with a dash and heavy rush, first from one quarter, then from another. I was watchful and faced each rush firmly braced. Generally, this preparedness saved me; but several times the wind apparently expanded or exploded beneath me, and with an upward toss, I was flung among the icy rocks and crusted snows. Finally I took to dropping and lying flat whenever a violent gust came ripping among the crags.

There was an arctic barrenness to this alpine ridge,—not a house within miles, no trail, and here no tree could live to soften the sternness of the landscape or to cheer the traveler. The way was amid snowy piles, icy spaces, and windswept crags.

The wind slackened and snow began to fall just as we were leaving the smooth plateau for the broken part of the divide. The next mile of way was badly cut to pieces with deep gorges from both sides of the ridge. The inner ends of several of these broke through the center of the ridge and extended beyond the ends of the gorges from the opposite side. This made the course a series of sharp, short zigzags.

We went forward in the flying snow. I could scarcely see, but felt that I could keep the way on the broken ridge between the numerous rents and canons. On snowy, icy ledges the wind took reckless liberties. I wanted to stop but dared not, for the cold was intense enough to freeze one in a few minutes.

Fearing that a snow-whirl might separate us, I fastened one end of my light, strong rope to Scotch's collar and the other end to my belt. This proved to be fortunate for both, for while we were crossing an icy, though moderate, slope, a gust of wind swept me off my feet and started us sliding. It was not steep but was so slippery I could not stop, nor see where the slope ended, and I grabbed in vain at the few icy projections. Scotch also lost his footing and was sliding and rolling about, and the wind was hurrying us along, when I threw myself flat and dug at the ice with fingers and toes. In the midst of my unsuccessful efforts we were brought to a sudden stop by the rope between us catching over a small rock-point that was thrust up through the ice. Around this in every direction was smooth, sloping ice; this, with the high wind, made me wonder for a moment how we were to get safely off the slope. The belt axe proved the means, for with it I reached out as far as I could and chopped a hole in the ice, while with the other hand I clung to the rock point. Then, returning the axe to my belt, I caught hold in the chopped place and pulled myself forward, repeating this until on safe footing.

In oncoming darkness and whirling snow I had safely rounded the ends of two gorges and was hurrying forward over a comparatively level stretch, with the wind at my back boosting along. Scotch was running by my side and evidently was trusting me to guard against all dangers. This I tried to do. Suddenly, however, there came a fierce dash of wind and whirl of snow that hid everything. Instantly I flung myself flat, trying to stop quickly. Just as I did this I caught the strange, weird sound made by high wind as it sweeps across a canyon, and at once realized that we were close to a storm-hidden gorge. I stopped against a rock, while Scotch slid in and was hauled back with the rope.

The gorge had been encountered between two out-thrusting side gorges, and between these in the darkness I had a cold time feeling my way out. At last I came to a cairn of stones which I recognized. The way had been missed by only a few yards, but this miss had been nearly fatal.

Not daring to hurry in the darkness in order to get warm, I was becoming colder every moment. I still had a stiff climb between me and the summit, with timberline three rough miles beyond. To attempt to make it would probably result in freezing or tumbling into a gorge. At last I realized that I must stop and spend the night in a snowdrift. Quickly kicking and trampling a trench in a loose drift, I placed my elkskin sleeping bag therein, thrust Scotch into the bag, and then squeezed into it myself.

I was almost congealed with cold. My first thought after warming up was to wonder why I had not earlier remembered the bag. Two in a bag would guarantee warmth, and with warmth a snowdrift on the crest of the continent would not be a bad place in which to lodge for the night.

The sounds of wind and snow beating upon the bag grew fainter and fainter as we were drifted and piled over with the later. At the same time our temperature rose, and before long it was necessary to open the flap of the bag slightly for ventilation.

At last the sound of the storm could barely be heard. Was the storm quieting down, or was its roar muffled and lost in the deepening cover of snow, was the unimportant question occupying my thoughts when I fell asleep.

Scotch awakened me in trying to get out of the bag. It was morning. Out we crawled, and, standing with only my head above the drift, I found the air still and saw a snowy mountain world all serene in the morning sun. I hastily adjusted sleeping bag and snowshoes, and we set off for the final climb to the summit.

The final one hundred feet or so rose steep, jagged, and ice-covered before me. There was nothing to lay hold of; every point of vantage was plated and coated with nonprehensile ice. There appeared only one way to surmount this icy barrier and that was to chop toe and hand holes from the bottom to the top of this icy wall, which in places was close to vertical. Such a climb would not be especially difficult or dangerous for me, but could Scotch do it? He could hardly know how to place his feet in the holes or on the steps properly; nor could he realize that a slip or misstep would mean a slide and a roll to death.

Leaving sleeping bag and snowshoes with Scotch, I grasped my axe and chopped my way to the top and then went down and carried bag and snowshoes up. Returning for Scotch, I started him climbing just ahead of me, so that I could boost and encourage him. We had gained only a few feet when it became plain that sooner or later he would slip and bring disaster to both. We stopped and descended to the bottom for a new start.

Though the wind was again blowing a gale, I determined to carry him. His weight was forty pounds, and he would make a top-heavy load and give the wind a good chance to upset my balance and tip me off the wall. But, as there appeared no other way, I threw him over my shoulder and started up.

Many times Scotch and I had been in ticklish places together, and more than once I had pulled him up rocky cliffs on which he could not find footing. Several times I had carried him over gulches on fallen logs that were too slippery for him. He was so trusting and so trained that he relaxed and never moved while in my arms or on my shoulder.

Arriving at the place least steep, I stopped to transfer Scotch from one shoulder to the other. The wind was at its worst; its direction frequently changed and it alternately calmed and then came on like an explosion. For several seconds it had been roaring down the slope; bracing myself to withstand its force from this direction, I was about moving Scotch, when it suddenly shifted to one side and came with the force of a breaker. It threw me off my balance and tumbled me heavily against the icy slope.

Though my head struck solidly, Scotch came down beneath me and took most of the shock. Instantly we glanced off and began to slide swiftly. Fortunately I managed to get two fingers into one of the chopped holes and held fast. I clung to Scotch with one arm; we came to a stop, both saved. Scotch gave a yelp of pain when he fell beneath me, but he did not move. Had he made a jump or attempted to help himself, it is likely that both of us would have gone to the bottom of the slope.

Gripping Scotch with one hand and clinging to the icy hold with the other, I shuffled about until I got my feet into two holes in the icy wall. Standing in these and leaning against the ice, with the wind butting and dashing, I attempted the ticklish task of lifting Scotch again to my shoulder—and succeeded. A minute later we paused to breathe on the summit's icy ridge, between two oceans and amid seas of snowy peaks.

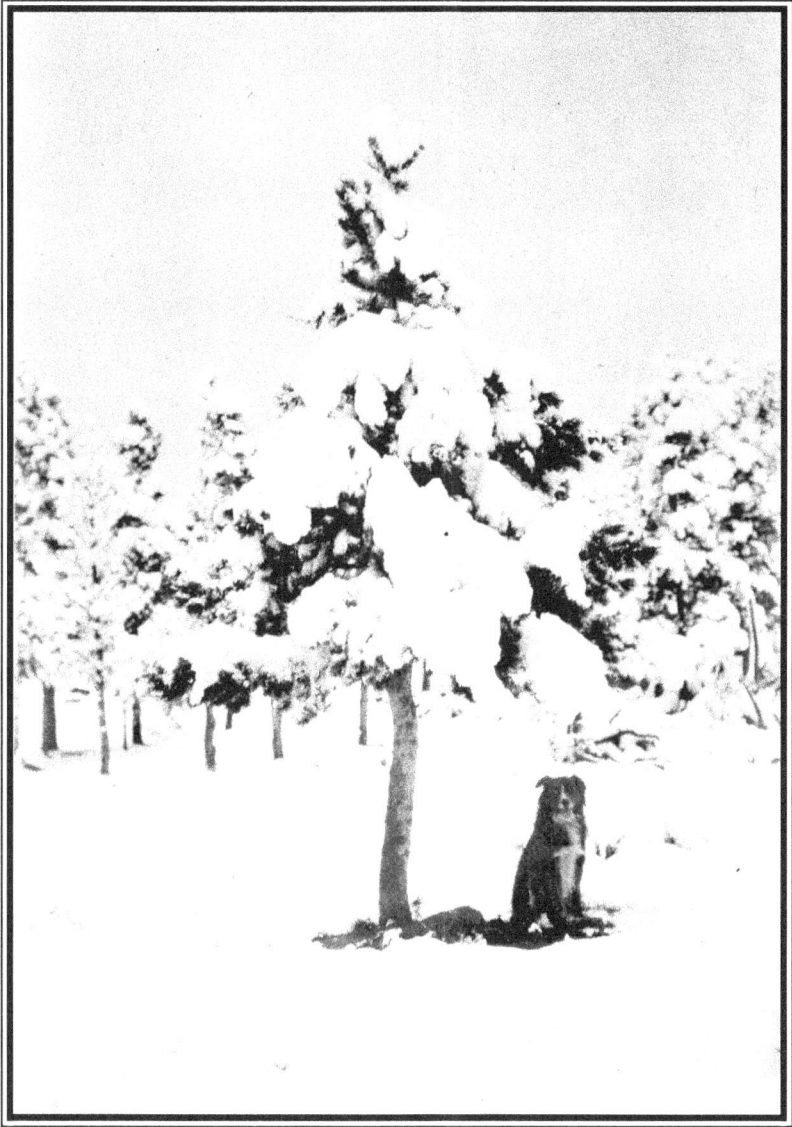

Scotch, Enos' border collie. For more of their adventures together, please see "Stories of Scotch" by Enos A. Mills.

All sorts of things and weather must be taken in together, to make up a year and a sphere.
Ralph Waldo Emerson

The Long Winter Sleep

When the food of the grizzly bear becomes scarce, he goes to bed and sleeps until a reasonable supply is available, even though he waits five months for it. He feasts on this fullness of the land during the summer and wraps himself in a thick blanket of fat. When winter comes on, he digs a hole and crawls in. This layer of fat is a nonconductor of cold and in due time is drawn on for food.

One autumn day I visited the Hallett Glacier with a professor from the University of Chicago. After exploring one of the upper crevasses, we stood looking down the steep slope of the glacier. New snow had fallen a few days before, and a soft, slushy coating still overlaid the ice. The professor challenged me to coast down the steep, snow-lubricated ice slope. We seated ourselves on this soft, slippery snow, and he gave the word "Go." Just as we slid away, we saw at the bottom of the slope, where we were soon to be, a huge grizzly bear. I wish you might have seen our efforts as we tried to change our minds on that steep slope! The grizzly was busily eating grasshoppers, but he heard us coming and fled at a racing gallop, giving an excellent exhibition of his clumsy hind legs reaching out flatfooted.

Each autumn numbers of insects and sometimes bushels of grasshoppers either are blown upon the ice and snow or else approach it too closely and fall from having their wings chilled. Evidently the grizzlies long ago learned of this food supply, for the ice fields are regularly visited by them during the autumn. Along the timberline the grizzly feeds freely upon the last of autumn's berries and the last green plants. Many a grizzly goes to the heights to put on fat for his long winter's sleep.

Bear food becomes scarce as winter approaches. Fruit, berries, grass, and weeds are out of season; most birds and insects are gone. The bear feeds on what remains—small animals which he digs out, a stray stranded fish, now and then a dead bird or animal carcass, the red fruit of the rose, and the nuts, bark, and roots of trees and plants. I do not believe the grizzly eats a special or a purgative food during the few days preceding his denning up, although he may do so.

On the few occasions when I have been able to keep track of a bear during the four or five days immediately preceding his retirement, he did not eat a single thing. I have examined a number of grizzlies that were killed while hibernating, and in every instance the stomach and intestines were empty. These facts lead me to conclude that bears rest and fast for a few days before going permanently to the winter den.

The bear generally prepares his winter quarters in advance of the time needed. He may occasionally sleep in his den before taking possession of it for the winter. But this is exceptional. In two cases that I know of he lay outside the den, though near it; and a number of other times he kept away from the den until he entered it for the long sleep. After the den is completely ready, the grizzly continues his usual search for food. Generally this requires long excursions and he may wander miles from the den.

In climbing along the bottom of a deep, narrow ravine one November day, I saw on the slope above me what appeared to be a carload or more of freshly dumped earth. My first thought was that a prospector was at work driving a tunnel; but upon examination it proved to be a recently finished but not yet occupied hibernating den. The entrance was about three feet in diameter. Just inside the den was a trifle larger. It extended, nearly level, about twelve feet into the mountainside. At the back it was six feet across and four feet high.

The size of the den varies and is apparently determined by the character of the soil in which it is made and also by the inclination of the bear making it. Most other dens measured were smaller than this one.

The grizzly may use the same den for several winters or have a new one each year. He may dig the den himself or take an old one that some other bear has used, or he may make use of one shaped by Nature—a cave or a rockslide. I knew of one grizzly hibernating in a prospector's abandoned tunnel. Sometimes, like the black bear, he will dig a den on a steep mountainside beneath the widely spreading roots of trees; sometimes beneath a large fallen log, close to the upturned roots which support it. In crossing the mountains one February I noticed a steamy vapor rising from a hole in the snow by the protruding roots of an overturned tree. I walked to the hole to investigate. The vapor was rank with the odor of a bear. Near my home on the slope of Long's Peak I have known grizzlies to den up beneath the snow-crushed, matted tree growths at the timberline, at an altitude of about eleven thousand feet.

Twice I have known bears to hibernate in enormous nests that were made of the long fibers of cedar bark. It must have taken days to construct one of these nests, as more than forty cedar trees had been more or less disrobed to supply material for it. It resembled the nests of trash that razorback hogs in the South construct, though much larger. The bear, after piling it up, worked his way in near the bottom, somewhat after the fashion of a boy crawling into a haycock. Over this hibernating nest the snow spread its blanket and probably afforded all the protection needed.

Sometimes the entrance to a den is partly closed by the occupant. Once in, he reaches out and claws the lower part full of earth, or rakes in trash and leaves. In most instances nothing is done to close the entrance. The snows drift back into the den, pile upward, and at last close the entrance most effectually.

All the dens that I recall were upon northerly or easterly—the cooler—slopes. The snow as it fell would be likely to remain and close or blanket the entrance all winter long. Snow evidently enters into the grizzly's winter plans.

Late one cold, snowless December I came upon a grizzly carrying spruce boughs into his den. Evidently he had used the den and found it cold. The den had a large opening; this he may have been intending to close. The rocky floor was already piled a food deep with boughs. I have seen two other dens with floor coverings; one of these was of pine twigs, and the other of coarse grass and kinnikinick. Though, in most cases the bear sleeps upon the uncovered rocks or the naked earth.

Snow is a factor in determining when a bear begins his winter sleep. If he is fat and food is scarce, and early, heavy snow is pretty certain to cause him to turn in early. If no snow comes and food is still to be had, the bear is likely to delay his hibernation.

The individual inclination of the bear and his condition—whether fat or thin—are also factors which influence his time of retiring. I knew of two bears, apparently of similar condition, one of whom turned in three weeks earlier than the other. Two bears whom I noticed one winter ran about more than a month after all the other bears had disappeared. Both were thin—just why I should like to know. They also turned in shortly after they became rounded out. Generally bears of a locality turn in for winter about the same time. Hibernating may begin early in November, but in most localities, and in most years, the time is likely to be a month later.

In Alaska and the Northwest many bears hibernate in the heights above the timberline. I have found a number in the mountains of Colorado with winter quarters at an altitude of twelve thousand feet. In southern Colorado and in the Yellowstone Park region many have denned up at about the altitude of six thousand feet. A grizzly may hibernate anywhere in his territory where he can find or make a den to his liking.

Except when there are cubs, a grizzly dens alone. Accounts which tell of a number of full-grown grizzlies spending the winter in one den lack verification. The cubs are born in the hibernating den, and they den up with the mother the first, and sometimes the second, winter after their birth. The cubs generally den up together the first winter after they are weaned.

Once in for the winter, the bear is likely to stay in the den for weeks. Most of the time probably is spent sleeping, and, so far as known, without either food or water. A bear may be routed out of his winter quarters without difficulty. Generally his sleep is not heavy enough greatly to deaden his senses. Hunters, trappers, floods, and snow-slides have driven grizzlies from their dens during every stage of hibernation, and in each case a moment after the bear came forth his senses were as alert as ever; he was able either to run away or to fight in his normal manner.

Prospectors in Jefferson Valley, Montana, told me of staking claims and starting to drive a tunnel early one December. A day or two after they began blasting they saw a bear break out of a snowy den and scamper away on the mountainside. They tracked him to the place where he had holed up again. It was their belief that the noise or the jar of their shots had awakened and reawakened the bear, until, disgusted, he left the region for an quieter sleeping place.

A sniffling and grunting attracted my attention one midwinter day as I was snowshoeing along the side of a ravine. Presently, a short distance ahead of me, I saw a grizzly's nose thrust out of a hole in the snowy slope. Then his head followed. Sleepily the grizzly half opened his eyes, then closed them again. His shaking and drooping head fell lower and lower, until with a jerk he raised it only to let it droop again. He repeated this performance a number of times. Evidently it was the head of a very sleepy grizzly. Occasionally he opened his eyes for a moment, but he did not seem interested in the outside world and he finally withdrew his head and disappeared in the den.

After midwinter, and especially towards spring, a bear sometimes comes out for fresh air and exercise, or to sun himself. One gray February day, snowshoeing along the Big South Poudre, I chanced to look across an opening from the edge of the woods and saw a grizzly walking round and round in a well-beaten pathway in the snow. Occasionally he reared up, faced about, and walked round in the opposite direction. His den was near by. Half a mile farther on I came upon a bear trail near the entrance to another den. Here the bear had walked back and forth in a pathway that was about sixty feet long. It was beaten down in the snow to a depth of fifteen inches. Two places showed that the bear had rolled and wallowed about in the snow.

Elsewhere, another year, about the middle of March, I examined much worn pathways near a grizzly's den. These had been made at least three weeks before and had been used a number of times. One pathway led to the base of a cliff that faced the east, where the bear had probably lain in the morning sun. Another led to a much used spot that caught the afternoon sun.

Perhaps a bear sometimes becomes tired or restless during his long winter sleep. Now and then he comes forth in the spring with the fur worn off his hips, back, or shoulders. He may kill time, when through sleeping, with a short excursion outside the den. If the den is large, he sometimes tramples about like a caged animal.

Climatic conditions, the altitude at which the bear hibernated, and other factors determine the time when grizzlies leave their dens. Most of them come forth during March, but stragglers may not appear until late in April. Mothers with cubs remain in the den a few weeks longer than bears without cubs.

At the limits of tree growth, one cold March day, I came upon the tracks of a grizzly bear descending the mountain. I backtracked them and found the den in which the grizzly had spent the winter. The inside of the den was gravelly and comparatively clean. Only this single line of tracks led from the den, though the weather had been clear for a week; so I judged this was the first time the grizzly had sauntered forth. It was just sundown when I reached the den. The heights were icy, and I hesitated about continuing across the Divide that night, so concluded to occupy the den. I knew that bears often take a short ramble in the spring and then return to the den, but I took the chances of sharing it with him. I do not know what the grizzly did that night—whether or not he came back. My fire in the mouth of the den may have kept him at bay.

The hard, cracked skin on the soles of the grizzly's feet is shed during hibernation, and the feet in spring are soft and tender. For several days he avoids traveling over rough places. His claws grow out during the winter rest, also. When he goes to sleep they are worn, broken, and blunt; but he comes out of winter quarters with claws long and moderately pointed.

What is the grizzly's condition in the spring after months of fasting? He has hibernated from three to five months, and in this time probably has taken neither water nor food. First of all he comes forth fat and not in the least hungry. The walls of his stomach have greatly contracted, almost completely closing the interior. Two stomachs which I saw taken from grizzlies killed early in the spring were as hard as chunks of rubber, and had capacity for not more than two or three spoonfuls. But when the grizzly reappears after his long winter sleep he is as strong as ever and can run for hours or fight with normal effectiveness.

He may not eat anything for a few days after leaving the den. For many days he eats lightly, and it may be two weeks before he has a normal appetite. His first food is likely to be the early, tender shoots of plants or trees, tuberous roots, swelling buds, and green grass.

I once watched a grizzly for seven days after he emerged from his hibernating cave. His winter quarters were near timberline on Battle Mountain, at an altitude of nearly twelve thousand feet. The winter had been of average temperature, but with scanty snowfall. I saw him, by chance, just as he left the den, on the first day of March. He walked about aimlessly for an hour or more, then returned to his sleeping place without eating or drinking anything.

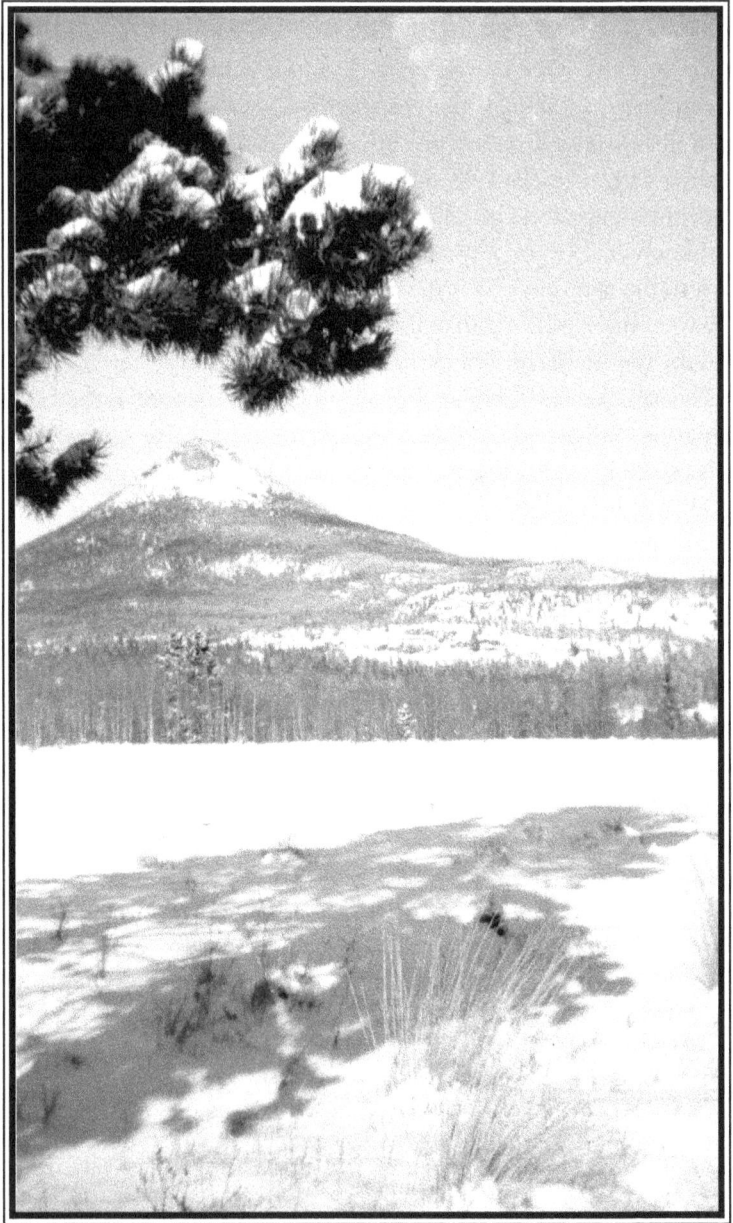

Estes Cone in winter.

The following day he wandered about until afternoon before he broke his fast. He ate a mouthful of willow twigs and took a taste of water. He walked leisurely down the mountain and towards sundown made himself a nest at the foot of a cliff in the woods. Here he remained, apparently sleeping, until late the next afternoon. Then, just before sundown, he walked out a short distance, smelled a number of things, licked the snow a few times, and returned to his nest.

The fourth day he went early for water and ate more willow twigs. In the afternoon he came upon a dead bird,—apparently a junco,—which he ate. After another drink he lay down at the foot of a tree for the night. The following morning he drank freely of water, surprised and devoured a rabbit, and then lay down. He slept until noon the next day, then set out foraging; he found a dead mouse and toward evening caught another rabbit. The seventh day was much like the preceding one. During the first week out the grizzly did not eat food enough to make him one ordinary meal.

Hibernation is not well understood. The habit probably originated from the scarcity of food. However, in Mexico grizzlies sometimes hibernate even though the climate be mild and food plentiful. As these grizzlies probably came from the cold north, the habit may have been fixed in the species when it arrived. Hibernation appears to be helpful and not harmful, and it may therefore continue for ages even though not required. The rest which hibernation gives to mind and stomach, with the entire organism relaxed, may both increase efficiency and lengthen life.

The polar bear has its own peculiar hibernating habits. The food of this bear is sea food. This is available even in the wintertime, on or beneath the ice. The male polar bears do not hibernate; the females do not except when about to give birth to young. The cubs at birth are small and helpless, and require the mother's constant care and the shelter of the den for some weeks after birth.

Mr. J. D. Figgins has written one of the best comments on hibernation that I have read. I quote as follows: —

"The period of hibernation in any mammal not only varies in a given species, but is largely influenced by the available supply of food to which it is accustomed or that is necessary for its requirements.

"Examples of this character may be cited among several species of mammals. It is the custom of the chipmunks, or 'ground squirrels,' to hoard up at least a partial supply of food in the autumn for consumption during the winter months; but this is rarely, if ever, sufficient to keep these interesting little animals active for the entire period. In most localities, there is no available food with which to augment their scant store and they are never in evidence from late October to April. In other locations where the fruit of the Crataegus, or 'thorn apple,' is to be had, they may be seen almost daily, although the ground may be covered with several feet of snow and low temperatures prevail.

"Another example is the opussum. Ordinarily these animals are active throughout the entire year, but towards the northern edge of their range they frequently hibernate for considerable periods (thirty-one days from personal observations).

"Certain of the small rodents can, and probably do, hoard sufficient food for actual need during the winter months; but the problem is in direct ratio to the size of the animal. Hence we find the marmot, a much larger animal, making no provision, although his habitat is confined to the higher altitudes and his period of hibernation is extended over a greater length of time than many other species. His food consists wholly of grass and other green plants, and it is doubtful if he could subsist on dry food. Granting that he could, the amount required would be prohibitive, otherwise he would make some effort in that direction, as do the conies, a much smaller animal.

"Being omnivorous and of great size, a bear could not secure or preserve the necessary amount of food to carry him through five months. Such food could not consist of any variety other than vegetation, and he is not a 'hay' eater, and so, nature has provided him a means of surviving the long period of fasting and probably, without discomfort.

"It is well known that bears show a distinct preference for fruit during the late summer and autumn months. Not because that is the season for the various fruits, but through a need of their sugar content and its fattening qualities. Composed largely of juices which are quickly absorbed, the digestive process is very brief and the discarded residue is discharged at once. This may give rise to the belief that a purgative has been employed as a means of cleansing the bowels and explains the presence of unbroken berries in the excrement and the absence of offensive odors. As a means of exploring the purgative theory we need only refer to bears in captivity. Although the latter may be confined to cement floors and have no access to any matter whatever, other than the food regularly supplied, they frequently hibernate in a quite orderly manner.

"It must be conceded that bears are irregular in the period of 'holing up' and that they do so only when food has become too scarce to sustain activities without a drain upon the store of fat they have acquired; or during very severe weather. In the mean time there has been a gradual reduction in food as the period of hibernation approaches and a consequent lessened activity of the bowels. Nor is there reason for surprise because of the absence of excrement in the burrow and the presence of matter in the rectum when the bear emerges in the spring.

"In captivity bears may, or may not, hibernate. As a rule they 'sleep' for more or less varying periods during severe weather. One authority states the grizzly has been known to sleep from sixty to seventy-five days and during that time it was not difficult to awaken him. Black bears frequently pass the winter without evidence of even drowsiness. Others awake at irregular intervals, and after feeding lightly, return to their slumber."

The winter life of many animals is stern and strange. During the autumn the beaver stores up a food supply for use when the pond is closed over with ice. The cony harvests hay for his winter food. Numbers of animals hunt food each day in the snow. But the woodchuck and the bear hibernate, that is, they fast and sleep in a den during the winter.

The proper function of man is to live not exist. I shall not waste my days in trying to prolong them. I shall use my time.
    Jack London

Racing an Avalanche

I had gone into the San Juan Mountains during the first week in March to learn something of the laws which govern snowslides, to get a fuller idea of their power and destructiveness, and also with the hope of seeing them in wild, magnificent action. Everywhere, except on windswept points, the winter's snows lay deep. Conditions for slide movement were so favorable it seemed probable that, during the next few days at least, one would "run" or chute down every gulch that led from the summit. I climbed on skees well to the top of the range. By waiting on spurs and ridges I saw several thrilling exhibitions.

It was an exciting experience, but at the close of one great day the clear weather that had prevailed came to an end. From the table-like summit I watched hundreds of splendid clouds slowly advance, take their places, mass, and form fluffy seas in valley and canyons just below my level. They submerged the low places in the plateau, and torn, silver-gray masses of mists surrounded crags and headlands. The sunset promised to be wonderful, but suddenly the mists came surging past my feet and threatened to shut out the view. Hurriedly climbing a promontory, I watched from it a many colored sunset change and fade over mist-wreathed spires, and swelling, peak-torn seas. But the cloud masses were rising, and suddenly points and peaks began to settle out of sight; then a dash of frosty mists, and my promontory sank into the sea. The light vanished from the heights, and I was caught in dense, frosty clouds and winter snows without a star.

I had left my skees at the foot of the promontory, and had climbed up by fingers and toes over the rocks without great difficulty. On starting to return I could see only a few inches into the frosty, sheep's wool clouds, and quickly found that trying to get down would be a perilous pastime. The side of the promontory stood over the steep walls of the plateau, and, not caring to be tumbled overboard by a slip, I concluded that sunrise

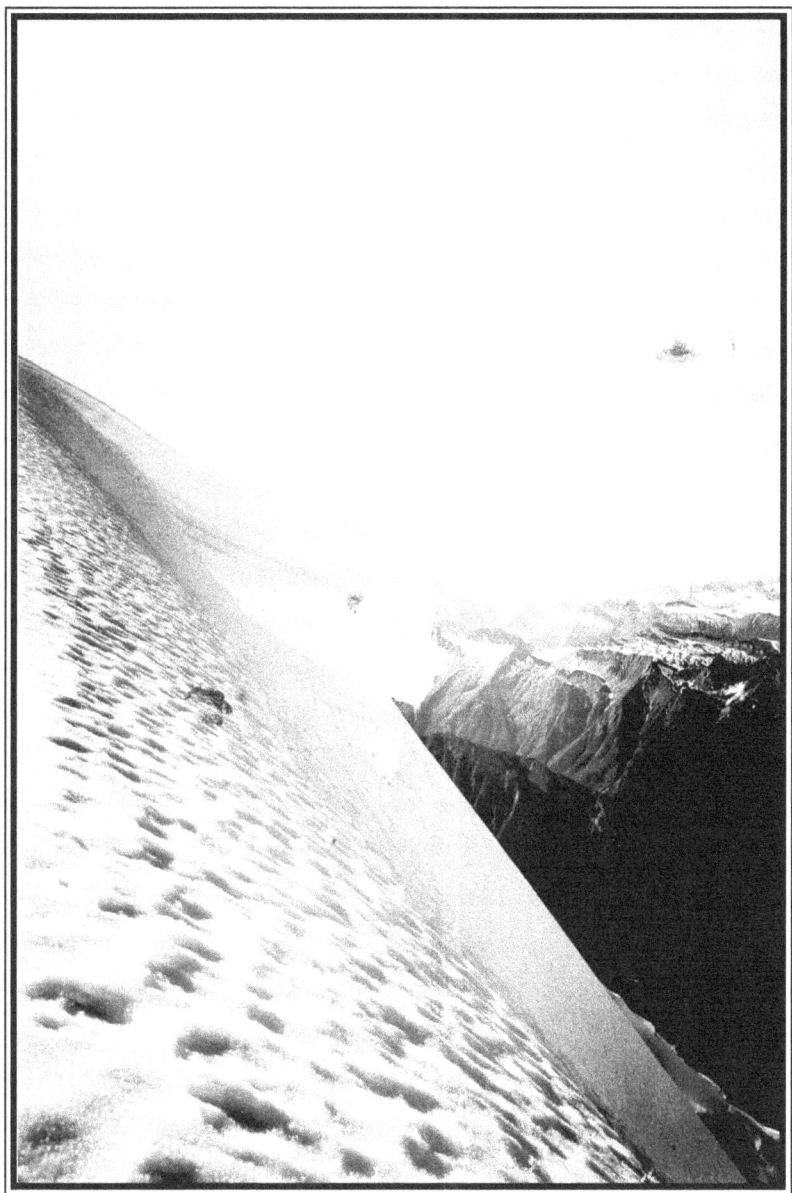

A snow cornice hangs over a valley, ready to run.

from this point would probably be worthwhile.

It was not bitter cold, and I was comfortably dressed; however, it was necessary to do much dancing and arm swinging to keep warm. Snow began to fall just after the clouds closed in, and it fell rapidly without a pause until near morning. Early in the evening I began a mental review of a number of subjects, mingling with these, from time to time, vigorous practice of gymnastics or calisthenics to help pass the night and to aid in keeping warm. The first subject I thought through was arctic explorations; then I recalled all that my mind had retained of countless stories of mountain climbing experiences; the contents of Tyndall's "Hours of Exercise in the Alps" was most clearly recalled. I was enjoying the poetry of Burns when broken clouds and a glowing eastern sky claimed all attention until it was light enough to get off the promontory.

Planning to go down the west side, I crossed the table-like top, found, after many trials, a break in the enormous snow cornice, and started down the steep slope. It was a dangerous descent, for the rock was steep and smooth as a wall, and was overladen with snow which might slip at any moment. I descended slowly and with great caution, so as not to start the snow, as well as to guard against slipping and losing control of myself. It was like descending a mile of steep, snow-covered barn roof,—nothing to lay hold of and omnipresent opportunity for slipping. A short distance below the summit the clouds again were around me and I could see only a short distance. I went sideways, with my long skees, which I had now regained, at right angles to the slope; slowly, a few inches at a time, I eased myself down, planting one skee firmly before I moved the other.

At last I reached a point where the wall was sufficiently tilted to be called a slope, though it was still too steep for safe coasting. The clouds lifted and were floating away, while the sun made the mountains of snow still whiter. I paused to look back and up, to where the wall ended in the blue sky, and could not understand how I had come safely down, even with the long tacks I had made, which showed clearly up to the snow-cornice, mist-shrouded crags at the summit. I had come down the side of a precipitous amphitheater which rose a thousand feet or more above me. A short distance down the mountain, the slopes of this amphitheater concentrated in a narrow gulch that extended two miles or more.

Altogether it was like being in an enormous frying pan lying face up. I was in the pan just above the place where the gulch handle joined.

It was a bad place to get out of, and thousands of tons of snow clinging to the steeps and sagging from corniced crests ready to slip, plunge down, and sweep the very spot on which I stood, showed most impressively that it was a perilous place to be in.

As I stood gazing upward and wondering how the snow ever could have held while I came down over it, there suddenly appeared on the upper steeps an up-burst as from an explosion. Along several hundred feet of cornice, sprays and clouds of snow dashed and filled the air. An upward breeze curled and swept the top of this cloud over the crest in an inverted cascade.

All this showed for a few seconds until the snowy spray began to separate and vanish in the air. The snow cloud settled downward and began to roll forward. Then monsters of massed snow appeared beneath the front of the cloud and plunged down the slopes. Wildly, grandly they dragged the entire snow cloud in their wake. At the same instant the remainder of the snow-cornice was suddenly enveloped in another explosive snow cloud effect.

A general slide had started. I whirled to escape, pointed my skees down the slope,—and went. In less than half a minute a tremendous snow avalanche, one hundred or perhaps two hundred feet deep and five or six hundred feet long, thundered over the spot where I had stood. There was no chance to dodge, no time to climb out of the way. The only hope of escape lay in outrunning the magnificent monster. It came crashing and thundering after me as swift as a gale and more all-sweeping and destructive than an earthquake tidal wave. I made a desperate start. Friction almost ceases to be a factor with skees on a snowy steep, and in less than a hundred yards I was going like the wind. For the first quarter of a mile, to the upper end of the gulch, was smooth coasting, and down this I shot, with the avalanche, comet-tailed with snow-dust, in close pursuit. A race for life was on.

The gulch down which I must go began with a rocky gorge and continued downward, an enormous U-shaped depression between high mountain ridges. Here and there it expanded and then contracted, and it was broken with granite crags and ribs. It was piled and bristled with ten thousand fire-killed trees. To coast through all these snow-clad obstructions at breakneck speed would be taking the maximum number of life and death chances in the minimum amount of time. The worst of it all was that I had never been through the place. And bad enough, too, was the fact that a ridge thrust in from the left and completely hid the beginning of the gulch.

As I shot across the lower point of the ridge, about to plunge blindly into the gorge, I thought of the possibility of becoming entangled in the hedge-like thickets of dwarfed, gnarled timberline trees. I also realized that I might dash against a cliff or plunge into a deep canyon. Of course I might strike an open way, but certain it was that I could not stop, nor see the beginning of the gorge, nor tell what I should strike when I shot over the ridge.

It was a second of most intense concern as I cleared the ridge blindly to go into what lay below and beyond. It was like leaping into the dark, and with the leap turning on the all-revealing light. As I cleared the ridge, there was just time to pull myself together for a forty-odd-foot leap across one arm of the horseshoe shaped end of the gorge. In all my wild mountainside coasts on skees, never have I sped as swiftly as when I made this mad flight. As I shot through the air, I had a glimpse down into the pointed, snow-laden tops of a few tall fir trees that were firmly rooted among the rocks in the bottom of the gorge. Luckily I cleared the gorge and landed in a good place; but so narrowly did I miss the corner of a cliff that my shadow collided with it.

There was no time to bid farewell to fears when the slide started, nor to entertain them while running away from it. Instinct put me to flight; the situation set my wits working at their best, and, once started, I could neither stop nor look back; and so thick and fast did obstructions and dangers rise before me that only dimly and incidentally did I think of the oncoming danger behind.

I came down the farther side of the gorge, to glance forward like an arrow. There was only an instant to shape my course and direct my flight across the second arm of the gorge, over which I leaped from a high place, sailing far above the snow-mantled trees and boulders in the bottom. My senses were keenly alert, and I remember noticing the shadows of the fir trees on the white snow and hearing while still in the air the brave, cheery notes of a chickadee; then the snowslide on my trail, less than an eighth of a mile behind, plunged into the gorge with a thundering crash. I came back to the snow on the lower side, and went skimming down the slope with the slide only a few seconds behind.

Fortunately most of the fallen masses of trees were buried, though a few broken limbs peeped through the snow to snag or trip me. How I ever dodged my way through the thickly standing tree growths is one feature of the experience that was too swift for recollection. Numerous factors presented themselves which should have done much to dispel mental procrastination and develop decision. There were scores of progressive propositions to decide within a few seconds; should I dodge that tree on the left side and duck under low limbs just beyond, or dodge to the right and scrape that pike of rocks? These, with my speed, required instant decision and action.

With almost uncontrollable rapidity I shot out into a small, nearly level glacier meadow, and had a brief rest from swift decisions and oncoming dangers. How relieved my weary brain felt, with nothing to decide about dodging! As though starved for thought material, I wondered if there were willows buried beneath the snow. Sharp pains in my left hand compelled attention, and showed my left arm drawn tightly against my breast, with fingers and thumb spread to the fullest, and all their muscles tense.

The lower edge of the meadow was almost blockaded with a dense growth of fire-killed trees. Fortunately the easy slope here had so checked my speed that I was able to dodge safely through, but the heavy slide swept across the meadow after me with undiminished speed, and came crashing into the dead trees so close to me that broken limbs were flung flying past as I shot down off a steep moraine less than one hundred feet ahead.

All the way down I had hoped to find a side canyon into which I might dodge. I was going too rapidly to enter the one I had seen. As I coasted the moraine it flashed through my mind that I had once heard a prospector say it was only a quarter of a mile from Aspen Gulch up to the meadows. Aspen Gulch came in on the right, as the now slightly widening track seemed to indicate.

At the bottom of the moraine I was forced between two trees that stood close together, and a broken limb pierced my open coat just beneath the left armhole, and slit the coat to the bottom. My momentum and the resistance of the strong material gave me such a shock that I was flung off my balance, and my left skee smashed against a tree. Two feet of the heel was broken off and the remainder split. I managed to avoid falling, but had to check my speed with my staff for fear of a worse accident.

Battling breakers with a broken oar or racing with a broken skee are struggles of short duration. The slide did not slow down, and so closely did it crowd me that, through the crashing of trees as it struck them down, I could hear the rocks and splintered timbers in its mass grinding together and thudding against obstructions over which it swept. These sounds, and flying, broken limbs cried to me "Faster!" and as I started to descend another steep moraine, I threw away my staff and "let go." I simply flashed down the slope, dodged and rounded a cliff, turned awkwardly into Aspen Gulch, and tumbled heels over head—into safety.

Then I picked myself up, to see the slide go by within twenty feet, with great broken trees sticking out of its side, and a snow cloud dragging above.

The snowflakes seemed larger and larger, at last they looked like great white fowls.

Hans Christian Anderson, "The Snow Queen"

The Ptarmigan at Home

The high-lying mountain plateaus are lands strangely full of life and romance. These magnificent distances up in the sky are a novel scene. Nowhere is there a solitary pine to check or tune the wild and heedless winds; it is a ragged-edged realm with numerous outreaching plateaus and mesas, without the sheltering, softening influence of grove or forest.

Walking among the stunted, half-buried trees at timberline one snowy, bright winter day, I narrowly escaped stepping upon a snow-white ptarmigan that had been squatting in its little hollowed out depression in the snow. It ran a short distance, then, squatting, became invisible. I startled a second ptarmigan, then a third, before realizing it must be a flock. Ten or fifteen rose at once with a loud cackle and flew high over the snow to an outjutting ridge. Their dazzling white bodies were impressively beautiful against the clear, bright blue winter sky.

Except in the nesting season, ptarmigan are most often seen in flocks. The ptarmigan, sometimes called "mountain quail," and the leucosticte, or rosy finch, are the highest ranging and most alpine of all birds in Colorado. Occasionally, during prolonged storms, they may descend below timberline even two or three thousand feet, but they are permanent residents of the heights. In these lower scenes they appear to have a rollicking vacation.

I once planned to get close to a flock of ptarmigan by going on all fours. They were in their summer garb and barely discernable as they moved quietly about their feeding ground. When within perhaps fifteen feet of them I stopped. They were coming towards me. Occasionally one snapped at a fly, ate a leaf, or grabbed a grasshopper. There were twenty-five or more in the flock. Presently all were around me. Three or four went beneath me, several passed close in front, and two in pursuit of something ran between my arms. They must have considered me a rock, if they even considered me. To them perhaps I was simply part of the topography.

They moved on so slowly that I finally became tired of being a quadruped. Glancing up, I saw two mountain sheep watching me closely from a nearby boulder pile. Evidently they could not classify me. The muscles of my neck and back ached, but I tried to hold my place until the ptarmigan were well out of the way. At last I allowed myself to slowly settle to the grass, where I stretched out at full length. I could not see where the sheep stood without moving; but I could hear the low clucking or conversation which the ptarmigan continually carried on.

Soon this conversation became more distinct. Evidently the entire flock was returning. While waiting I watched a high soaring eagle. He must have been three thousand feet above me, and where I lay the altitude was nearly thirteen thousand feet. As he circled lower, his shadow rushed across nearby rocks where a marmot, sunning himself, gave a clear, scolding whistle and fled.

In summer the marmot population above timberline is a numerous one. His shrill whistle, like a traffic policeman's, penetrates the unobstructed distances with an inquiring "Who goes there?" He seldom waits for an answer. Before you approach he scrambles awkwardly off his boulder and disappears into his den. He is of a darker color than his lowland cousin, the woodchuck or ground hog, but has the same habits of taking long sunbaths throughout the summer and hibernating during winter. One marmot at Keyhole on the Long's Peak trail has shared many a lunch with climbers who tarried at this point to await the return of their party from the ascent to the top. Food and patience, sitting quietly, will bring almost any wild thing into our acquaintance.

I had flattened myself out on the ground waiting for the flock of ptarmigan. Something must have frightened them. They came running past my feet and head. Two leaped upon me, followed by others. One jumped off on the opposite side, but the rest stood for a few seconds, looking about, not considering me at all. Then all but one stepped off and went slowly forward. The last one walked along my side and for a moment used my shoulder for a viewpoint. Then he came stamping over my head and cheek before leaping down into the low-growing grass. Then he turned for a look at me as though it had just occurred to him that I might be something alive. Being unable to decide, he turned and went leisurely on, considering only his own affairs. When I rose, the ptarmigan were out of sight. The word "ptarmigan" is probably from the Gaelic "tarmachan," meaning "mountaineer." The ptarmigan is found on the highest windswept hills of the British Isles, on the snowy summits of the Rocky Mountains as far south as the Taos range in northern New Mexico, around the Arctic Circle, on the long chain of the Aleutian Islands, and across the Arctic tundras of North America from Labrador to western Alaska.

In Colorado it breeds from eleven thousand feet to the summit of many high peaks and winters at timberline. It feeds on the buds of dwarfed willows in winter. In summer it adds grasshoppers, caterpillars, beetles, and other insects which the alpine plants support to its diet of leaves, grasses, and flowers.

The ptarmigan nests above timberline among the jagged rocks and boulders, the nest being merely a depression on the ground, lined with a little grass or leaves or a few feathers. Finding such a nest is almost pure accident, for if the ptarmigan has attained the utmost protection for itself in its concealing plumage and slow movements, it has gone still further in concealing its nest.

I was watching two ptarmigan, wondering if they had a nest somewhere near. In the midst of the watching a mountain sheep and her two little lambs appeared on a ridge nearby. I turned to watch them for perhaps half a minute. A cliff of rocks rose behind the ptarmigan, and a ridge of boulders barred one side of them. As I stood in the open before them, I felt that even while watching the sheep the ptarmigan could not get away without my knowing it.

When I turned to look for them, they were nowhere to be seen. I was certain that they had not flown away. I advanced to the spot where I had last seen one of them and stood looking all around. Then I made a series of concentric circles, examining the ground closely. Not locating either of the birds, I returned to the spot where one had been. I had about decided to give up the search, when one of them commenced to peck my shoe. I was standing so close that I was actually touching her with my toe.

On another occasion a ptarmigan rose for a short distance and lighted. I walked to the spot and searched and searched without finding it.

I sat down on a boulder, looked about, wrote notes, and looked about some more. In the midst of this waiting a gust of wind blew my hat off. In grabbing for the hat I nearly struck the ptarmigan, which was sitting patiently on a nearby boulder, waiting for me to leave first.

Remarkable changes of plumage take place twice a year, this semiannual moult providing the bird with perfect concealment from its enemies at any season. In winter, when its range is mostly snow covered, it is robed in pure white, even to its feathered legs and feet. Its bill and eyes are shining black. At other seasons its mottled brown and gray and white plumage blends so perfectly with the gray-brown granite rocks and scattered patches of dirty snow that it is almost impossible to locate.

The ptarmigan has mastered the fine art of living in regions seemingly uninhabitable. But even with its perfect adaptation of dress, it has much to contend with from the fox, bear, lion, and weasel. The weasel, or ermine, has its own white winter suit, which serves as an advantage to it in securing its prey in the same degree that the ptarmigan's white dress is beneficial. Around mining camps the ptarmigan has been considerably reduced in numbers because of its edibility, and because of its utter lack of fear making it comparatively easy to catch.

In wandering the bleak, snowy heights in winter I came to love this rare bird. Often as I passed near a flock on snowshoes, they would watch me silently but at the same time with confidence and seeming satisfaction. They are the silent birds of the silent peaks. Their few, brief calls are hoarse and strange. They cannot be translated into English words. The notes are generally of inquiry or alarm. On rare occasions a number of these birds will join in a brief, rattling chorus which suggests the efforts of the guinea. The call of the male bird slightly resembles the call of a turkey. The quiet movements and silence of this alpine bird make its presence very impressive to the lonely visitor. I have never met beast or bird that is so expressive in the language of silence. They dearly want to be intimate, but they never say so. The ptarmigan has won my heart wherever I have found it among the crags or on the small willow-dotted tundras. Its deliberateness, its self-containedness, and its bold life among the wild, lonely scenes combined to give me a strong attachment for it.

The ptarmigan enjoys the wild mountain blizzards, and in the headlong whirl of the snow it is as much at home as a duck on the waves.

In running it generally goes forward with a series of spurts and pauses, the frequency and duration of these pauses decreasing as the speed is increased. It flies but little, but when its wings are used, its manner of flight is very like that of the prairie chicken.

In June or early July the proud mother ptarmigan leaves her rude nest on the ground and struts about with from six to fifteen lively little cotton balls. The young ptarmigan grow up among some of the most beautiful and healthful scenes on earth. They live on the very roof of the world. The alpine meadows which they ramble are scattered with snowdrifts and strewn with bright flowers.

Donald MacMillan in "Four Years in the White North" has the following record of ptarmigan: "Common at Etah in spring and fall migration. Not seen in July and August. Undoubtedly many remain in far North throughout the year. Seen on March 19, 1914, when we were crossing the Beitstadt Glacier of Ellesmere Land at a height of 4,700 feet, with a temperature of $50°$ F. These birds pick through the crust of snow with their bill, then clear away loose snow with their feet, in order to uncover willow buds. The breeding note in April resembles very much the sound of a policeman's rattle. Nesting date early in June."

Stefansson in "The Friendly Arctic" has several references to ptarmigan, the following in Lougheed Island (at the extreme edge of the Arctic Ocean): "The summer brought but one flock of ptarmigan and the ducks were only king eiders and old squaws. Plovers probably do not go that far north but there were sandpipers, snow buntings, owls, and the same three kinds of gulls noted farther north. It goes without saying that there were no signs of Eskimos."

Hudson Stuck in "The Ascent of Denali" (Mount McKinley) makes the following comment: "at this camp (ten thousand feet) at the head of the glacier we saw ptarmigan on several occasions, and heard their unmistakable cry on several more, and once we felt sure that a covey passed over the ridge above us and descended to the other glacier. It was always in thick weather that these birds were noticed at the glacier head, and we surmised that perhaps they had lost their way in the cloud.

"But even this was not the greatest height at which bird life was encountered. In the Grand Basin, at sixteen thousand, five hundred feet, Walter was certain that he heard the twittering of small birds familiar throughout the winter in Alaska, and this also was in the mist. I have never known the boy make a mistake in such matters, and it is not essentially improbable. Doctor Workman saw a pair of choughs at twenty-one thousand feet, on Nun Kun in the Himalayas."

The ptarmigan and the rosy finch together possess these treeless heights of the Rockies the year round. One cold, snowy day I took shelter under a rock cliff and found a flock of rosy finches had found this refuge ahead of me. Quietly, almost gladly, they allowed me to share their shelter from the storm. They nest as high as thirteen thousand feet, upon the rocks.

The treeless area in the San Juan mountains of Colorado is unusually impressive. In it, the sky prairie is well grassed, comparatively level and smooth, and it is one of the highest and possibly the highest, tableland of like area in the world. It reposes at about thirteen thousand feet. It is surrounded by a magnificent nearby wall of rugged peaks and commands splendid views down into the surrounding valleys.

Mountaintops have comparatively little snowfall. Often during a snowstorm, as well as during a rainstorm, the region above the timberline is above the storm line. The region of greatest snowfall is the middle slopes of the mountains; the mountaintops in most localities have a comparatively dry climate. The yearly weather story of the alpine heights is one of the most interesting in weather lore. Go to the summits for sunshine. The air is clear. Everything is serene. Night after night on the heights stars crowd as nowhere else.

Peaks have their storms, but in all my experience I know of their being struck by lightning only a few times. Often, however, the air of the heights is surcharged with electricity while a storm is below. Wonderful are the terrific winds of the high plateaus. They sometimes boom and roar for hours, beating against the crags and rushing through passes, with a speed of more than one hundred miles an hour. Occasionally, while exploring two miles above the sea, I watched a storm come to the world below. The peak's slopes were encircled and the lowlands covered. Subdued thunders rolled and echoed beneath the clouds; their upper surface—their silvery lining—broke and rolled around rocky headlands like the sea, and there were brilliant rainbows in the scenes below, while high peaks stood thoughtful in the sunlight.

Enos and Scotch
explore frozen Chasm
Lake on Long's Peak.
Photographs by
Dean Babcock.

From the heights one sees the cloud scenes—clouds large and small—clouds like detached high mountains and low, wide plains—come and go. One sees close at hand the under sides of clouds, their edges, slopes, peaks, canyons, and summits.

The utter absence of trees in the heights gives a desert effect and makes it a strange world by itself. Timberline in the Rockies is the wavering and far reaching shore of the vast forest sea that lies deep and wide over the irregular surface of the mountains below. And also it is the shoreline of the treeless, island-like lands that stand above it. This treeless realm is not a solid mass, but appears an archipelago in the sky, made up of many long, large, deeply indented islands, with small outlying islands in clusters and isolated ones off by themselves. Stretches are extensive tablelands, cut with a few short deep canyons and piled with picturesque buttes. Other areas are occupied by peaks that tower in clusters or extend to the horizon in single file.

There areas above eleven thousand, five hundred feet are a numerously populated life zone in summer, and have grasslands, fields of wild flowers, and many birds and animals to their highest points. There are places, acres in extent, deeply overlaid with rich soil, and countless spaces and patches of soil at the foot of cliffs, on ledges, in boulder fields, and between shattered rock fragments. Wherever soil is found, it is pretty certain in summer to be covered with sedges, grasses, and brilliant wild flowers—flowers of red, yellow, blue, and orange; flowers on tall, slender stalks in the shelter of boulders and rock crevices; and low-growing dwarfed blossoms that cling to the earth almost stemless.

Many an eternal snowfield has a fringe of colored bloom. Around it bees hum, and here butterflies with intentionally pretty wings add decoration and charm. These varicolored gardens are of as many sizes and forms as the silken cloud shadows that are so strangely, definitely projected against the alpine land.

There are matted growths of arctic willow and dwarfed black birch along the alpine streams. Here many visiting birds nest and sing. Many birds, probably the majority of species, raise two broods each year. They may build a new nest for the second brood. In the Rockies the white-crowned sparrow and the broad-tailed hummingbird nest early among the mid-slope flowers, at nine thousand feet or lower, and then move up the slope two or three thousand feet higher to be among the alpine flowers and insects while the second brood of children grow up. Summer comes later to the heights, and they are able to raise both broods of children in its warmth and in the midst of abundant food supply. Here the paintbrush is at its reddest—a favorite with mountain hummingbirds.

The mountain nesting habits of these and other species have often led me to wonder if there may not be lowland birds, who, after hatching one brood, travel several hundred miles farther into the north and raise the second family. In most places a thousand feet of altitude supplies many of the conditions given by a thousand miles of latitude. The complications which these mountains introduce, the numerous varieties of birds found in a small area, and the other features which they maintain, give increased interest to the whole story of bird life and travels.

The temperature and climatic conditions of these heights being somewhat similar to those of the polar world of the Arctic, they appeal to many of the same species of birds and plants. Some species of birds, of the same kind that nest in the Far North, come to this mountain realm from the far southland and use it for their summer nesting place; while others, who winter in the lowlands of these mountains, make the short migratory flight of an hour or less up the slopes and there, above the timberline, nest and raise their young. These few birds have a short, easy, migratory journey, but they must miss a most interesting experience. I cannot imagine anything more delightful than the journey most birds have in the long migratory flight from the southland to the Arctic Circle of the mountain heights, and then the return journey when the autumn colors paint the land.

One June I camped at twelve thousand feet, just above the timberline. Late in the evening I heard the robins and the solitaires singing in the woods below. Near me the ptarmigan and the rosy finches conversed and called to their kind. In a brook before my camp I saw an ouzel, and a pair of white-crowned sparrows hopped about among the dwarfed willows. Other summer bird neighbors of the ptarmigan are the American pipit and the junco.

On a dry moor back of camp I saw a Wilson's warbler, a horned lark, and a Savannah sparrow. One night a long-eared owl flew silently by. Among the birds that evidently were just flying visitors from the woods below, were the alpine three-toed woodpecker, the Western bluebird, one of the fly catchers, and a number of noisy Clark nutcrackers.

The presence of a woodpecker above the limits of the woods occasioned a mild surprise. A greater surprise to me was a visit from the camp-robber—the Rocky Mountain gray jay. This species lives in the seclusion of the deep woods and rarely does it venture far into the open. Perhaps he espied my camp; the instinct of this bird to visit the camps of people is simply irresistible. Although they sometimes come for company or to satisfy curiosity, the chief motive is for food. This visitor eagerly lunched with me. Perhaps he came with this expectation.

Each autumn wildlife congregate to feast and frolic in the heights. To this feast come little and big fellows in their furs and many a bird of fine feathers. There are birds and beasts of prey to fatten on the feasters. There are a few thousand birds. Many come a thousand miles or more from the North; others come up the mountainside a few thousand feet. Many live in the neighborhood, or are cradled in nearby scenes. They are resting, playing, and exploring. When the colored leaves are falling, the birds young and old go far away to the warm southland. The winds and snows make merry in the scenes where they loved and sang and happily raised their children for their brief, adventurous life. What, I wonder, are the thoughts of the ptarmigan when the sweet, uneasy note of the bluebird tells of southland dreams?

In this strange, alluring mountaintop world I have spent many a week, in winter and in summer, camping along the alpine streams and exploring rocky peaks. Always there was life around me, birds and animals leading their busy, happy lives beyond the front ranks of the forest.

This treeless realm is overspread with a million silvery rootlets of several mighty rivers. Beautiful lakes, with rocky boundaries, are scattered along the farthest edge of the forest. Around these lakes many birds gather, to drink and bathe and to feed. Sit beside any lake or stream and you will have innumerable glimpses of bird life. Whether they nest near by or afar, birds will come to rest and play, or perhaps—who knows?—just to visit.

170

Top of Long's Peak in Winter
Climbing to the Clouds With High Diet.

He will not see me stopping here
  To watch his woods fill up with snow.
      Robert Frost

The Bighorn in the Snow

One winter morning an old mountain sheep came down from the heights through the deep snow and called at my cabin. We had already spent a few years trying to get acquainted. Most of these slow advances had been made by myself, but this morning he became a real neighbor, and when I opened the door the Master of the Crags appeared pleased to see me. Although many a shy, big fellow among the wild folks had accepted me as a friend, I had not even hoped to have a close enough meeting with a wild a wild bighorn ram to make an introduction necessary for good form.

I stood for a moment just outside the cabin door. The situation was embarrassing for us both; our advances were confusing, but I finally brought about a meeting of actual contact with bighorn. With slowness of movement I advanced to greet him, talking to him all the while in low tones. Plainly his experiences assured him that I was not dangerous, yet at the same time instinct was demanding that he retreat. For a time I held him through interest and curiosity, but presently he backed off a few steps. Again I slowly advanced and steadily assured him in the universal language—tone—that all was well. Though not alarmed, he moved off at right angles, apparently with the intention of walking around me. I advanced at an angle to intercept him. With this move on my part, he stopped to stare for a moment, then turned and started away.

I started after him at full speed. He, too, speeded, but with snow-shoes I easily circled him. He quickly saw the folly of trying to outrun me; and if he did not accept the situation with satisfaction, as I think he did, he certainly took things philosophically. He climbed upon a snow-draped boulder and posed as proudly as a Greek god. Then he stared at me.

Presently he relaxed and showed a friendly interest. I then advanced and formally introduced myself, accompanying my movements with rapid comment and chatter. I asked him if he was glad to be alive, asked his opinion concerning the weather, the condition of his flock, and finally,

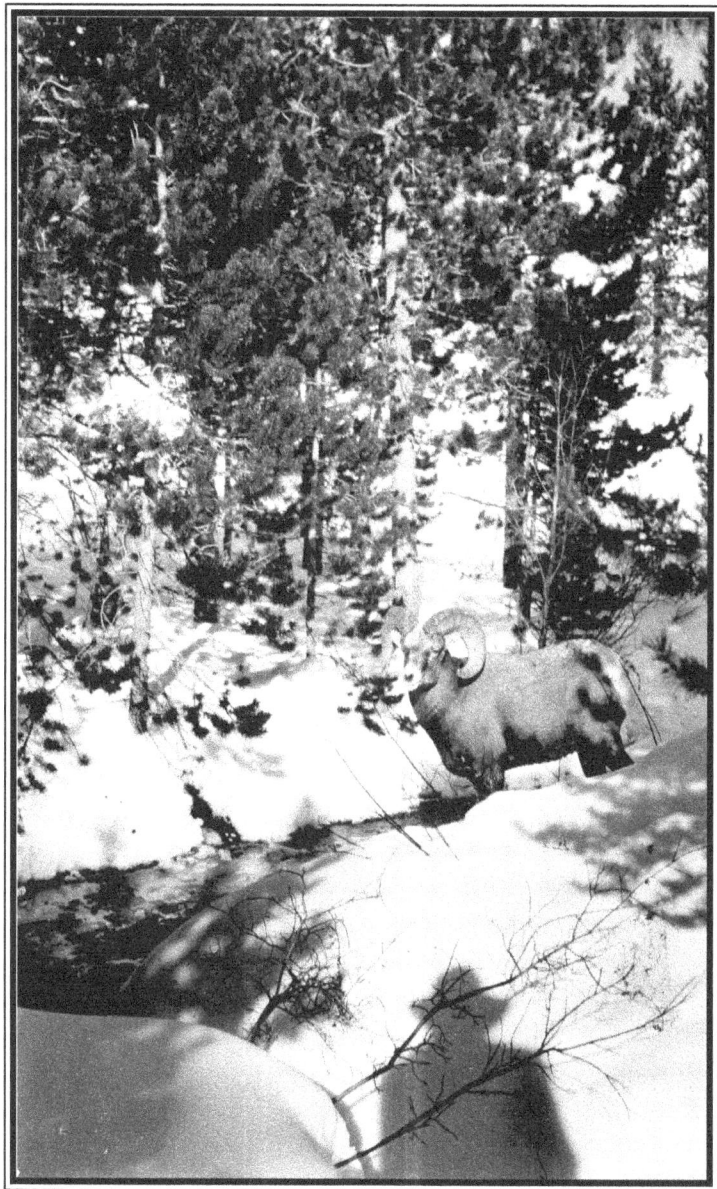

Enos visits with his Bighorn sheep neighbor.

told him that game preserves was one of my hobbies, and in such refuges I trusted he had a deep interest. All this, while within a few yards of him and in a most friendly tone; still he remained almost coldly curious.

At last I begged the rare privilege of taking his picture, and as he was not in a place for good picture taking, I proceeded to drive him to a spot closer to my cabin. To my astonishment he was willingly driven! He went along as though he had often been driven and as though going to a place of which he was fond!

Among scattered pines and willows by my brook I circled him and took a number of photographs. At last I walked up to my bighorn friend, rubbed his back and felt his horns. He was not frightened but appeared to enjoy these attentions, and to seem proud of my association. But, my big speechless fellow, I had the most from your call!

Twice afterward, once in the winter and once midsummer, he called and came up to me, and with dignified confidence licked salt from my hand. In the Sierras and the Rocky Mountains there are numerous flocks of bighorn or wild mountain sheep which have a resident stamping ground above the timberline, at an altitude of 12,000 feet. They appear not to migrate, although they go often into the lowlands; in spring for the earliest green stuff, in summer for salt or for a change, and during the winter when conditions commend or command such a move. With the coming of a storm or if there is an attack on them, they at once climb high among the crags, up close to where the eagles soar.

The heights thus is the home of wild sheep. The young are born in bare places among the crags and the snowfields. All stand the storms up close to the sky. They are warmly wrapped; their long, coarse outer coat of hair is almost waterproof and defies the cold.

One of my trips as Snow Observer carried me across the wild Continental Divide while the sky was clearing after a heavy snowfall. In climbing to the summit I passed close to three herds of deer that were stranded in deep snow. But the high wind had swept the treeless summit, and in places the snow had been deeply excavated. In other places it had been thrown into massive drifts. On the summit plateau at an altitude of 12,000 feet I rounded a crag and came close upon a flock of mountain sheep in the moorland from which the wind had swept most of the snow. The sheep were bunched, scattered, and a few were lying down. Here in the heights the sheep had already forgotten the storm, while the elk and the deer far down in the wooded slopes were deeply troubled by the snow. With this open place on the mountain top, these hardy dwellers of the summit could long be indifferent to deep snow or to its deliberate melting.

They bunched in the farthest corner of their wind-cleared place and eyed me curiously while I went by. I backtracked their wallowed trail to the nook in which they had endured the three day storm. This place was nearly a mile distant, but over most of the way to the snowless pasture the sheep had traveled on the very edge of the plateau, from which wind and gravity had cleared most of the snow. They had stood through the storm bunched closely against a leeward plateau wall several yards below the summit. The snow had eddied down and buried them deeply. It had required a long and severe struggle to get out of this snow and back through it to the summit, as their footmarks and body impressions plainly showed.

This storm was a general one and deeply covered several states. It was followed by two weeks of cold. For several hundred miles along this and other ranges the deer and the elk had a starving time, while the numerous flocks of sheep on summits escaped serious affliction.

Evidently mountain sheep know their range and understand how to fight the game of self-preservation in the mountain snows. The fact that sheep spend their winters on the mountain summits would indicate that they find a lower death rate and more comfort here that they could find in the lowlands.

The morning I started across Sawtooth Pass the snow was deep. A gray sky and a few lazily falling snowflakes indicated that it might be deepened. And soon the flakes were falling fast and the wind was howling. Only between gusts could I see. But on I went, for it was easier to advance than to retreat.

I passed over the summit only to find the wind roaring wildly on the other side. Abandoning the course of the snow-buried trail, I went with the wind, being extremely careful to keep myself under control lest the breezes boost me over an unexpected cliff. The temperature was a trifle below zero, and I watched nose, fingers, and cheeks to keep them from freezing.

Two violent gusts drove me to shelter beneath a shelving rock. After half a minute a long lull came and the air cleared of snow dust. There within thirty feet of me were a number of mountain sheep. Two were grazing in a space swept bare by the wind. Another was lying down, not in shelter, but out in an exposed place.

Then I caught sight of two lambs and I failed to see what the other sheep were doing. Those lambs! They were in a place where the wind hit violently, as the bare space around them showed. They were pushing each other, butting their heads together, rearing up on their hind legs. As I watched them another gust came roaring forward; they stopped for a second and then rushed toward it. I caught my last glimpse just as it struck them and they both leaped high to meet it.

I was in the heights when a heavy snow came down and did not drift. It lay deeply over everything except pinnacles and sharp ridges. I made a number of snowshoe trips to see how sheep met this condition. During the storm one flock had stood beneath an overhanging cliff. When the snowfall ceased the sheep wallowed to the precipitous edge of the plateau and at the risk of slipping overboard had traveled along an inch or less wide footing for more than a mile. Where the summit descended by steep slope they ventured out. Steepness and snow weight before their arrival, perhaps with the assistance of their tramplings, had caused the snow at the top to slip. As the slide thus started tore to the bottom it scraped a wide swath free of snow. In this cleared strip the sheep were feeding contentedly.

Snowslides, large and small, often open emergency feeding spaces for sheep. Long snowshoe excursions on the Continental Divide have often brought me into the presence of mountain sheep in the snow. They are brave, self-reliant, capable, and ever alert for every advantageous opportunity or opening.

One snowy time I searched the heights for hours without finding any sheep. But in descending I found a number upon a narrow sunny ledge that was free from snow; the trampling and the warmth of the sheep probably had helped clear this ledge. Here they could find scanty ration for a week or longer. I could not make out whether they had spent the storm time here or had come to it afterward.

In the heights are numerous ledges and knife-edge ridges on which but little snow can lodge. The cracks and niches of these hold withered grass, alpine plants, and moss, which afford an emergency food supply that often has saved snowbound sheep.

Sheep are cool-headed fellows, as well befits those who are intimately associated with precipices. But one day, while slowly descending a steep slope, I unintentionally threw a flock into confusion. Bunched and interested, they watched me approach within sixty or seventy feet. I had been close to them before and this time while moving closer I tried to manipulate my camera. An awkward exhibition of a fall resulted. The sheep, lost in curiosity, fled without looking where they leaped. The second bound landed them upon an icy pitch where everyone lost footing, fell, and slid several yards to the bottom of the slope. All regained their feet and in regular form ran off at high speed.

Accidents do befall them. Occasionally one tumbles to death or is crushed by falling stone. Sometimes the weaker ones are unable to get out of deep snow. On rare occasions a mountain lion comes upon them and slays one or several, while they are almost helpless from weakness or from crusted snow. A few times I have known of one or more to be carried down to death by a snowslide.

While the sheep do not have many neighbors, they do have sunny days. Often the heights, for long periods, are sunny and snowless. Sometimes a storm may rage for days down the slopes while the sheep, in or entirely above the upper surface of the storm cloud, do not receive any snow. Among their resident neighbors are the cony, the white weasel, the flocks of rosy finches and white ptarmigan. In these the sheep show no interest, by they keep on the watch for subtle foxes, bobcats, and lions.

Snowfall, like rainfall, is unevenly distributed. At times a short distance below the snow-piled heights one or both slopes are snowless; at other times, the summits are bare while the lowlands are overburdened with snow. Sheep appear quickly to discover and promptly to use any advantage afforded by their range.

One winter five sheep were caught in the lowlands by a deep snow. They had started homeward with the coming of the storm but were fired on by hunters and driven back. Becoming snowbound they took refuge in a springy opening at the bottom of a forested slope. This open spot was not a stone's throw across. It was overspread by outpouring spring water which dissolved most of the snow. Here the sheep remained for several weeks. This place not only afforded a moderate amount of food, but in it they had enough freedom of movement successfully to resist an attack of wolves. Apparently wolves do not attack sheep in their wintry heights. Deer and elk as well as sheep have often made a stand in a springy place of this kind.

Sheep under normal conditions are serene and often playful. There appears to be most play when the flock is united. Commonly they play by twos, and in this play butt, push, feint, jump, and spar lightly with horns, often rising to the vertical on hind legs. If a bout becomes particular lively the others pause to look on. They give attention while something unusual is doing. One day I saw a flock deliberately cross a snowdrift when they could easily have gone around it. But the sheep were vigorous from good feed and a mild winter and this snowdrift was across the game trail on which they were slowly traveling.

No wild animal grass eater excels the bighorn sheep in climbing skill, alertness, endurance, and playfulness. They thrive on the winds and rations of the heights. Generally the sheep carry more fat when spring comes than the deer that winter down in the shelter of the woods or in the lowlands. Any healthy animal, human or wild, who understands the wood craft of winter lives happily when drifts the snow.

Long's Peak in Winter.

www.ingramcontent.com/pod-product-compliance
Lightning Source LLC
Chambersburg PA
CBHW020705270326

41928CB00005B/272